THE MUSIC LIBRARY

The Instruments of Music

Stuart A. Kallen

LUCENT BOOKS
A part of Gale, Cengage Learning

 GALE
CENGAGE Learning™

Detroit • New York • San Francisco • New Haven, Conn • Waterville, Maine • London

LIBRARY OF CONGRESS CATALOGING-IN-PUBLICATION DATA

Kallen, Stuart A., 1955-
   The instruments of music / by Stuart A. Kallen.
     pages cm -- (The music library)
   Includes bibliographical references and index.
   ISBN 978-1-4205-0946-5 (hardcover)
1. Musical instruments--Juvenile literature. I. Title.
ML460.K25 2013
784.19--dc23
                        2012050540

Lucent Books
27500 Drake Rd
Farmington Hills MI 48331

ISBN-13: 978-1-4205-0946-5
ISBN-10: 1-4205-0946-2

CONTENTS

Foreword 4

Introduction
The Sounds of Music 6

Chapter 1
Percussion 9

Chapter 2
Woodwinds 26

Chapter 3
Brass 44

Chapter 4
Strings 60

Chapter 5
Keyboards 83

Chapter 6
Digital Instruments 100

Notes 118
Recommended Listening 121
Glossary 128
For More Information 130
Index 132
Picture Credits 136
About the Author 136

FOREWORD

In the nineteenth century, English novelist Charles Kingsley wrote, "Music speaks straight to our hearts and spirits, to the very core and root of our souls. . . . Music soothes us, stirs us up . . . melts us to tears." As Kingsley stated, music is much more than just a pleasant arrangement of sounds. It is the resonance of emotion, a joyful noise, a human endeavor that can soothe the spirit or excite the soul. Musicians can also imitate the expressive palette of the earth, from the violent fury of a hurricane to the gentle flow of a babbling brook.

The word *music* is derived from the fabled Greek muses, the children of Apollo who ruled the realms of inspiration and imagination. Composers have long called upon the muses for help and insight. Music is not merely the result of emotions and pleasurable sensations, however.

Music is a discipline subject to formal study and analysis. It involves the juxtaposition of creative elements such as rhythm, melody, and harmony with intellectual aspects of composition, theory, and instrumentation. Like painters mixing red, blue, and yellow into thousands of colors, musicians blend these various elements to create classical symphonies, jazz improvisations, country ballads, and rock-and-roll tunes.

Throughout centuries of musical history, individual musical elements have been blended and modified in infinite ways. The resulting sounds may convey a whole range of moods, emotions, reactions, and messages. Music, then, is both an expression and reflection of human experience and emotion.

The foundations of modern musical styles were laid down by the first ancient musicians who used wood, rocks, animal skins—and their own bodies—to re-create the sounds of the natural world in which they lived. With their hands, their feet, and their very breath they ignited the passions of listeners and moved them to their feet. The dancing, in turn, had a mesmerizing and hypnotic effect that allowed people to transcend their worldly concerns. Through music they could achieve a level of shared experience that could not be found in other forms of communication. For this reason, music has always been part of religious endeavors, from ancient Egyptian spiritual ceremonies to modern Christian masses. And it has inspired dance movements from kings and queens spinning the minuet to punk rockers slamming together in a mosh pit.

By examining musical genres ranging from Western classical music to rock and roll, readers will find a new understanding of old music and develop an appreciation for new sounds. Books in Lucent's Music Library focus on the music, the musicians, the instruments, and on music's place in cultural history. The songs and artists examined may be easily found in the CD and sheet music collections of local libraries so that readers may study and enjoy the music covered in the books. Informative sidebars, annotated bibliographies, and complete indexes highlight the text in each volume and provide young readers with many opportunities for further discussion and research.

The Sounds of Music

The Greek philosopher Plato once wrote: music "gives a soul to the universe, wings to the mind, flight to the imagination, a charm to sadness. . . . [It] leads to all that is good, just, and beautiful."[1] Plato's words, written around 2,400 years ago, demonstrate the transformative power and universal appeal of music.

In the most basic terms, music is sound transmitted by vibrations traveling through the air. It can be a songbird chirping in a tree, a cicada rubbing its hind legs together, a person singing in the shower, a rock group playing to a screaming audience, or a DJ "scratching" old records on a turntable. Above all, music communicates emotion, whether it comes from the serenely peaceful sound of a single wooden flute or the manic, angry hammering of a heavy metal band. Whether the music is coming from a lone performer or a one-hundred-piece symphony orchestra, instruments act as extensions of the feelings, inspirations, and spirits of the musicians playing them.

At its most basic level, music is sound waves that vibrate and interact with one another as they travel through the air. Although these waves can be re-created, it is said that, like snowflakes, no two musical performances are exactly alike. The same may be said of musical instruments. Composed of wood, metal, animal skin, plastic, or parts of plants, each instrument vibrates at a slightly different pitch and timbre, and with subtle variations of tone. Even two seemingly identical guitars of the same model and manufacturer will add slightly different colorations to the sound of music. This is why some people are as interested in collecting musical instruments as they are in playing them.

Often made from materials that were once alive, such as spruce, goat skin, or bamboo, musical instruments are extensions of nature. The sounds played upon them may remind listeners of leaves rustling in the breeze, an animal bleating in the forest, or the rumbling of thunder on the horizon. Those made from brass, plastic, or computer chips resonate with their own range of sound and texture, invoking the high spirits of the city after midnight, or even the noises of a spaceship landing in a field.

Humans have made musical instruments since the beginning of civilization. This marble figure of a man playing a lyre—a type of harp—was made by the Cycladians, a prehistoric culture of the Aegean Sea. It is nearly five thousand years old.

The physical components of individual instruments have long wielded influence over the sound of music. While it is hard to separate instruments from musicians, percussion, winds, brass, keys, and strings are tools that have influenced the music people have composed over the centuries. Thousands of years ago, when ancient societies had access only to drums and the human voice, music embodied the sounds of the tribal beat. In the age of Wolfgang Amadeus Mozart and Ludwig van Beethoven, popular music reflected the exhalations of the violin, cello, oboe, clarinet, and trumpet of the symphony orchestra. Today, guitars, drums, and synthesizers are used to express the wide range of emotions found in modern society. The fury of a young rock singer would be much harder to demonstrate to a large audience without an electric guitar blaring through a wall of screaming amplifiers. Likewise, the catchy hooks and trance-like beats made on keyboard synthesizers define the sound of the digital dancehall in the twenty-first century.

Above all, instruments are extensions of what composers, songwriters, and musicians hear inside their heads and feel in their souls. As Beethoven wrote across the top of his renowned Ninth Symphony, "From the heart it came, from the heart may it go."[2] Musicians continue to deliver Beethoven's vision by artfully employing the sounds of the piano, violin, cello, clarinet, oboe, flute, trumpet, and dozens of other instruments. Whether it comes from a single instrument or the combined sounds of an orchestra, music has the power to emotionally move listeners.

CHAPTER 1

Percussion

Music, unlike any other art form, takes place in time, and the steady rhythm of a song is like a heartbeat. A painting may hang on a wall for a thousand years, but live music passes in a matter of minutes. Music and time are intertwined, because it is the rhythm that keeps a song moving on its proper course. Musical rhythm may be held by the clapping of hands, the bounce of a bow across violin strings, the thumping of a bass guitar, or even the crash of waves on a beach. It is the rhythmic vibrations of drums and percussion instruments, however, that most often hold music's place in time.

At its most basic level, a percussion instrument is anything that produces a sound when hit with a hand or other implement such as a stick or mallet. The simplest percussive instruments are sticks, rocks, or other natural objects pounded together. Percussive instruments may also be hit with various devices. Bells are rung by the center clapper swinging back and forth. Xylophones are hit with rubber mallets. Rattles rely on shaken beads, gravel, or ball bearings. Bass drums are pounded with drumsticks. The Tibetan damaru is shaken rapidly, causing a knotted chord to thrum on both sides of a drumhead.

Idiophones

Whatever their form, percussive devices are the oldest instruments and date back twenty millennia or more. Percussion instruments that do not have to be tuned, such as gongs, castanets, triangles, and woodblocks, are called idiophones. These instruments resonate and are played by striking, scratching, scraping, rubbing, and shaking.

The first idiophones were made from rocks, sticks, animal skulls, antlers, bones, seashells, and plants such as dried gourds whose seeds rattled when shaken. Their rhythmic patterns, especially when established by more than one player, had the ability to change the mood of the listeners and urge them to get up and dance. As such, idiophones were originally played by shamans and religious practitioners, and their music had a deep religious significance. Mickey Hart, who played drums with the Grateful Dead for thirty years, describes the primeval spiritual connection to percussion instruments:

> We have idiophones dating back to 20000 B.C. that are daubed with red ochre [paint], a decoration most scholars believe indicates a sacred usage. But the first "document" of percussion's connection with the sacred doesn't show up until . . . around 15000 B.C., when an anonymous artist, working in a limestone cavern in southwestern France, painted our first known picture of a musician. Known as the dancing sorcerer (or shaman) of Les Trois Frères . . . this picture has been interpreted by scholars as representing a man wearing the skin of an animal and playing some kind of instrument, possibly . . . a concussion stick.[3]

Idiophones such as woolly mammoth skulls and bighorn sheep antlers are believed to have been pounded to generate good luck before a hunt. Gourd rattles might have blessed a baby's birth. The slow rhythm of a stick clacking across a ridged stone surface may have helped send a fallen warrior into the afterlife.

In the ancient tradition, idiophones can be anything that can be played rhythmically, including the human body. In the Amazon rain forest, indigenous tribes still perform a ritual fire dance while slapping their legs with their hands.

Natives of the Andaman Islands near India accompany traditional dances with a sounding board lying on the ground supported on one side by a rock and stamped with the heel of the foot. Nearly every culture on Earth has some sort of idiophonic device, whether simple or complicated, as Hart writes:

> In Papua New Guinea you'd hear the "clap clap" of shells and crayfish claws, while in Zaire the Vili [tribe] would slap the thick expanse of their thighs with hollowed out [gourds]. . . . Bwop . . . Bwop. The San [people] of South Africa fill springbok ears with pebbles and wear them on their ankles. In West Africa the top of a gourd is removed and the player pounds the open end against the ground, producing a nice percussive pop! as the trapped air vibrates against the fruit's tough skin. The gourd can be kept intact and beaten with sticks or chopped in half, placed hollow down in the water, and struck. In northern Haiti players put metal thimbles on their fingers to excite the gourd's

Idiophones are percussion instruments that do not have to be tuned and that can be played rhythmically, such as this East African balafon.

body, while in the Solomon Islands topless gourds are plunged in and out of water, making a sound that one writer transliterates as "uh/ah/ uh/ah/uh/ah."[4]

The Bells

While percussionists have used natural objects to play traditional music for tens of thousands of years, bells were not used in music until around 2000 B.C. when the Egyptians incorporated them into their songs. Bells are cup-shaped idiophones made from wood or metal, which contain a clapper that strikes the body of the device to produce a ringing sound. The clapper might also be a handheld object such as a drumstick.

Some types of modern African music, such as soukous, rely on the driving ring of funnel-shaped double bells to keep rhythm in large bands. The constant ring of the bell acts as a time-keeping metronome—like a conductor in a symphony orchestra—to keep the musicians on the beat.

Another type of African double bell, the agogo, has traveled around the world and been adapted by cultures on several continents, as drummer and music journalist Töm Klöwer explains:

> Black iron bells are predominantly played in African music, in places such as Togo, the Cameroons, Nigeria, and the Congo. . . . They were taken to the Caribbean and Brazil by the Bantus (who call the instrument "ngonge," which means "time and respect"), and the Yorubas (who call it "agogo"), as part of their African culture. The agogo is used in the Brazilian [religious] rituals, as well as in Brazilian street samba. This bell is characterized by a clear, bright sound, rich in harmonics.[5]

The wooden agogo, used in samba music, is similar to the metal version, but has a softer, more soothing tone. The cowbell, a more common type of bell, can be seen attached to rock-and-roll drum kits throughout the world. In recent decades, rock drummers have also added various bells commonly used in Latin American salsa music.

Groups of small bells may be incorporated into a single

idiophone. The traditional sleigh bells, associated with Christmas and the song "Jingle Bells," consist of around twenty-five small bells attached to a stick or a leather strap. Similar in sound, wrist and ankle bracelets originated in India are worn today by belly dancers, stage performers, and even rock bands.

Rattles

Rattles, like bells, were common in ancient cultures throughout the world. The first rattles were made from plants, small woven baskets, animal teeth, seashells, and plant seeds—a custom that continues today. Rattles are also central to indigenous Native American rituals, as music scholar Bernard S. Mason explains:

> Rattles are almost . . . indispensable to dancing in the eyes of most Indian tribes. . . . They are as universal among the Indians as . . . drums and usually hold a place of prestige almost equal to that of the drum. Not all dances call for rattles but some rituals cannot be performed without them; in fact, some use no drums at all, the only sound being the clicking of the rattles in the hands of the dancers.[6]

The most common rattles are made from dried gourds, but rattles may also be assembled from buffalo horns, birch bark, seashells, coconuts, and even tin cans. These instruments are filled with gravel, seeds, teeth, and other rattling devices. The exteriors of the rattles may be painted with symbolic designs, decorated with intricate beadwork, or have feathers or animal hair attached.

Rattles have religious significance for many people across the globe. In Korea, Buddhist priests attract gods by striking rattles with small sticks. In Brazil, indigenous people believe that the gods live within certain rattles. In Lapland (northern Scandinavia), traditionalists say the devil dwells in rattles. The importance of rattles in African healing ceremonies is explained by drum authority James Blades:

> The rattle is an important item of the equipment used by the African [healer]. During the operation of ejecting an evil spirit, the "medicine" man and his assistant

shake their rattles and growl throughout the whole performance, in order to terrify the spirit and render the patient more susceptible to the uncanny influence of the ceremony. On occasions of this nature the illusion is often intensified by the use of rattles adorned with fetishes or the carved head of a supernatural being, while the various complaints are treated with separate rhythms.[7]

Another common rattle, the maraca, was first named in a creation story from Guinea. It is believed that the goddess Crehu gave a calabash gourd and white pebbles to a tribesman and told him to put the gravel into the gourd and call it a maraca. That word has followed the rattling instrument around the world where maracas are used by traditional musicians, Latin American orchestras, and rock bands alike.

Valuable Gongs

Like rattles, gongs have been used for centuries throughout the world for religious purposes. In their simplest form,

Buddhist monks participate in a festival in northern India. Gongs and cymbals have figured in their religious ceremonies for centuries.

gongs are metal discs that resonate a single long, reverberating note when struck with a stick, mallet, or other device. The cymbals that rock drummers use are based on the ancient gong that originated in Southeast Asia around the ninth century.

Gongs have summoned Buddhists to meditation for centuries, and some museums display gongs that are nearly one thousand years old. Drummer Charles L. White describes ancient beliefs concerning gongs:

> Drinking from a gong bound a man to his oath. Washing oneself in a gong assured good health. The gong could frighten away evil spirits, cure the sick, bring favorable winds. Certain gongs were held in such high esteem that they were given proper names. Fine gongs were high in value . . . and they were considered a sign of wealth and rank. They have been used as currency.[8]

In the eighteenth century, gongs imported to the West from China were played in symphony orchestras. Gongs may be heard today in a wide variety of venues ranging from the dance music of India to the recordings of rock bands such as Pink Floyd, Led Zeppelin, Queen, and Aerosmith. In 2007, the Flaming Lips, an alternative-rock band, featured a gong during live performances of the song "Mountain Side."

Speaking with Slit Drums

While idiophones are the most ancient of instruments, drums did not appear until around 4500 B.C. Like bells, rattles, and gongs, however, drums have been used for a wide variety of purposes, from the mystical to the militaristic.

The earliest drums were most likely made from logs. Instruments called slit gongs, or slit drums, were used to send messages across the African jungle until recent times. Slit drums are hollowed-out logs that range from 3 feet to 40 feet in length (1m to 12m) with long slits carved into the top. Various vertical cuts along the slit give each drum a unique musical tone when they are beaten with mallets. As Blades writes, "The double note of the early log drums was

The Slit Drum Bush Telegraph

In Africa, slit drums were long used to send messages over great distances. Drum scholar James Blades explains this method of communication:

In remote parts of Central Africa, the signals transmitted by means of a drum language (Bush Telegraph) consist of a form of Morse code. Strokes of differing strength and pitch provide a form of "telephonic" conversation, by which news travels at considerable speed. The drum languages are as numerous as the almost innumerable languages and dialects of Africa itself. The early explorers were confounded by the obvious advanced knowledge of their movements over large areas. . . .

Certain slit drums are used solely for the purpose of transmitting messages from one . . . village or tribe to another. The telegraphists frequently beat their drums from a hill top, or from a floating raft. The resonance and carrying power of some of these instruments is remarkable. . . . The slightest flick of a finger produces a low boom. A blow with a beater so intensifies the volume that the sound is audible—to the trained ear, and under reasonable conditions—for a distance ranging from five to seven miles . . . though it is claimed that given certain favorable conditions certain drums are audible over a distance of twenty miles.

James Blades. *Percussion Instruments and Their History.* London: Faber and Faber, 1974, pp. 45–46.

probably one of man's first steps in instrumental melody."[9] Like other ancient instruments, slit drums are imbued with magical beliefs, and the hollowed-out slits where the tones emerge are considered home to deities, the dead, or sons yet unborn.

The Power of the Drum

Slit drums are considered idiophones because they do not have tunable drumheads. Most other drums, including modern drums, are classified as *membranophones* because the drumheads are made from animal skins, called membranes, which are stretched across the ends of hollow cylinders. The earliest drumheads were small instruments made from the skins of fish, lizards, and snakes. Tanned hides from rabbits, sheep, goats, pigs, mules, cows, dogs, or even wolves came into fashion in later centuries. The membranes are stretched taut and held in place by rope, leather cords, tacks, metal frames, or screws. These can be tightened or loosened to tune the instrument.

Drum cylinders might be hollow tree stumps, clay bowls, seashells, or even human skulls—any device that resonates and amplifies the sound when the skin is hit. Common drum shapes include the cone and double cone, the hourglass, the goblet, the barrel, and the bowl-shaped kettledrum. To those who love to drum, covering a cylinder with a membrane was an important step in human history. As

Tribesmen in Burundi, Africa, play traditional membranophones— drums made with animal skins. The African continent has the widest diversity of drums in the world.

Hart writes, "For me the discovery of the percussive possibilities of skin ranks right up there with the discovery of fire and the invention of the wheel."[10]

Mesopotamian art shows that simple clay drums existed five thousand years ago. Primeval female figurines found in Mesopotamia around 2300 B.C. show women playing small, round-frame drums similar to the tambourine. Music historian Layne Redmond describes such instruments:

The ancient frame drum . . . is primarily a wheel-shaped drum whose diameter is much wider than the depth of its shell. . . . The frame drum most often has a skin on only one side but sometimes it may have skins stretched across both sides. . . . Bells or jingling and rattling implements may be attached to the inside rim, and in ancient times were believed to add to the drum's power to purify, dispel, and summon. The drums were often painted red, the color of blood, or sometimes green, the color of vegetation. Throughout the ancient world, these were the primordial colors of life. Mystical designs and symbols might also be painted on the skin head or the wooden frame. Threads or ribbons knotted with ritual prayers or chants often hung from them.[11]

Over the centuries, membranophonic drums have been developed on nearly every continent, and at least fifty different types can be found in places such as Asia, Brazil, the Middle East, and North America. The African continent has more kinds of drums than any other. As Blades writes, "Every [tribe] inhabiting the vast territory has . . . had a drum of some description during its history. No indigenous musical instrument remains as widely spread or as greatly used."[12]

Those who could play drums with skill were elevated to leadership positions within tribes, as the instruments were thought to cure disease or inflict pain and bad luck. Ceremonies such as rain dances, hunting rituals, and war councils were conducted to the beat of the drum.

The Conga

With such a long history, drums have been made in every conceivable size and shape, from the towering, 15-foot-tall

(4.5m) African war drum to the tiny tambourine no bigger than a human hand. Common cylinder shapes include the cone and double cone, the hourglass, the goblet, the barrel, and the bowl-shaped kettle. Drums are also made

Battle Drums in Ancient Times

Drums have long been used to signal soldiers about the beginning of battle. In 1287, Italian explorer Marco Polo witnessed a battle between the armies of Mongol warrior Kublai Khan and that of his rival Nayan. Polo describes the battle, beginning with the sound of huge, 5-foot-tall kettledrums known as Naccara:

[When] all were in battle array on both sides . . . and nothing remained but to fall to blows, then might you have heard a sound arise of many instruments of various music, and of the voices of the whole of the two hosts loudly singing. For this is a custom of the [Mongols], that before they join battle they all unite in singing and playing . . . a thing right pleasant to hear. And so they continue in their array of battle, singing and playing in this pleasing manner, until the great Naccara (giant battle drums) of the Prince is heard to sound. As soon as that begins to sound the fight also begins on both sides; and in no case before the Prince's Naccara sounds dare any commence fighting. So then, as they were thus singing and playing, though ordered and ready for battle, the great Naccara of the Great Khan began to sound. And that of Nayan also began to sound. And thenceforward the din of battle began to be heard loudly from this side and from that. And they rushed to work so doughtily with their bows and their maces [and] with their lances and swords . . . that it was a wondrous sight to see.

Marco Polo. *The Travels of Marco Polo.* Taradale, Scotland: Amy Frances Yule, 1902, pp. 1081–1082.

in three basic styles: the single-head, closed at the bottom; the single-head, open at one end; and the double-head with skins on each end. The African kettledrum is an example of a single-head, closed-bottom drum. The bongo is a single-head drum open at one end. Single-head, closed-bottom drums include snares, tom-toms, and other drums found on modern drum sets.

Some of the most common drums in use today have roots in Africa. The conga, a single-head, barrel-shaped drum popular with salsa, rhythm and blues, rock, and jazz musicians, descends from the African makuta drums of the Congo region. With their ability to create an irresistible dance beat, congas play an important role in Latin music. They may be heard on street corners where carnival groups perform rumba and samba music, and on concert stages where superstars such as Shakira and Enrique Iglesias belt out pop Latino hits.

Players can coax various expressive sounds from congas by hitting the drumheads in various ways with their hand or arm. Striking the drum with the palm produces a bass note, while hitting with closed fingers produces a brighter sound called an open tone. Conga players can change the pitch of a single strike by quickly pressing an elbow into the drumhead after it is struck. Players might even push a wet finger across the drumhead to produce a loud squeaking tone.

A three-drum set known collectively as congas adds a bass-toned tumba, which is similar in shape but larger than a conga, and the higher-pitched quinto. Quality congas are made from hardwoods, although some modern drums are made from fiberglass and plastic. The drumhead is tanned cow or donkey hide from one-sixteenth to one-eighth of an inch thick. The heads can be tuned—that is, their pitch may be changed—by tightening or loosening screws attached to both the drum body and the metal tension ring that holds the skin in place.

Kettledrums and Timpani

While conga drums have mostly remained in the realms of Latin and rock music, kettledrums have had the distinction of crossing the cultural barrier from Africa, India, and the Middle East to western Europe in the sixteenth century. Kettledrums started out as single-head instruments with tightly stretched skins fitted over clay or copper bowls. Enlarged kettledrums were adapted by military drummers in India, as White explains:

> Some of the early kettle-shaped drums used by the tribes of India were made of pine wood hollowed out into hemispheric form and then equipped with heads of bull hide. Inside the wooden shell of these ancient Hindu drums were fitted bells of bronze. The drum was held high in the air and beaten in a loud and terrifying manner during battles, for the purpose of frightening the enemy. The bells were jingled by hitting [them] against the side of the drum. This was thought to create magic and bring good luck and victory.[13]

By the fifteenth century, kettledrums accompanied all royal parades in India. Bands that played for the emperor used massive instruments whose heads were about 5 feet (1.5m) in diameter and stretched across huge silver bowls weighing nearly 450 pounds (204kg) each. A single bull elephant was used to carry two of the drums and two drummers, each wielding his own pair of silver drumsticks used to pound out a loud, rumbling explosion of rhythm. Smaller drums were mounted on each side of a camel's humps while one drummer sat in the middle and played both pieces of equipment.

When the kettledrum was brought to Europe by Arab traders in the sixteenth century, European military leaders, like their Eastern counterparts, recognized the value of the thundering drums for warfare. As such, their popularity quickly spread across the continent from Germany to Russia and Great Britain.

The kettledrum eventually diminished in size to resemble the modern tambour, or timpani. These smaller drums were adopted by symphony orchestras in the eighteenth century after classical composers such as Johann Sebastian Bach and George Frideric Handel began writing for the kettledrum. According to White, the roaring crescendo of

An orchestra musician plays timpani, an instrument developed in Southeast Asia that arrived in Europe in the sixteenth century.

Handel's "Hallelujah Chorus" is "one of the most thrilling and effective parts ever written for the kettledrum."[14]

In a modern orchestra, the timpani player, or timpanist, plays three drums whose heads measure 24, 26, and 29.5 inches (61, 66, and 75cm) across. The drums have pedals that are depressed by the drummer's foot to change the tones with the music. The drums are struck with timpani sticks fitted with wooden, leather, cork, or hard felt balls on the end.

Jazzing up Drum Sets

Until the twentieth century, drums were mostly used for religious and ceremonial purposes or, in the case of timpani, to accompany classical music in the West. All that changed with the invention of jazz music in New Orleans, Louisiana, around the end of the nineteenth century. The first jazz musicians were African Americans who blended the music of ragtime, marching bands, and blues into an entirely new musical style.

Jazz was always driven by strong rhythms, and the first jazz bands had two drummers. One played a snare drum—a round, double-head drum, with a snare consisting of strands of wire, silk, or animal sinew stretched across the bottom head. The snare drum provides a sustained rattle, or "sizzle" sound when hit. The other drummer in a jazz band played a big bass drum and cymbal. The bass drum is a large two-head instrument originally worn around the neck while marching in parades. The playing surfaces are held perpendicular to the ground so the drummer can use mallets in both hands to pound out beats on the two drumheads.

Because most jazz musicians were poor, drummers could not afford fancy equipment and were often forced to improvise drum kits to keep up with the ever-changing styles of music. These early jazz players put together a drum kit that contained a number of instruments including a snare drum, several small bass drums called tom-toms (cylindrical single- or double-head drums), and a few cymbals. These drums originated in various regions throughout the world, as Hart explains:

> Drummers began ransacking the percussive inventory . . . [taking] elements from all over the planet— snares and bass drums from Europe, the tom-tom from China, cymbals from Turkey—and along with such homely additions as cowbells, anvils, and woodblocks invented a new kind of drumming and, incidentally, a new instrument.[15]

Early jazz drummers were limited to playing drums with only their hands and arms. This changed around 1920 when jazz drummer Warren "Baby" Dodds invented the drum foot pedal. This addition, which allowed drummers to use their foot to keep the beat on the big bass drum, was soon standard equipment on every kit.

Drum kits continued to evolve in the 1920s, when Zildjian, a Turkish cymbal manufacturer that had been in business for almost five hundred years, began selling its instruments throughout the United States. Drummers could now easily purchase what are known as crash and sizzle cymbals (named for their tone) and ride cymbals (which are continually tapped, or ridden). In 1926 drummer and inventor Barney Walberg created the final addition to the modern drum kit. He added two 13-inch (33cm) cymbals to a pedal-operated stand, or hi-hat, and the modern drum kit was complete. Drummers could now use one foot on the hi-hat and the other on the bass pedal to keep steady beats while adding accents and flourishes on other drums and cymbals.

Less than half a century after the first jazz drummers held down the beat with crude bass and snare drums, technically proficient drummers could use modern drum kits to execute complex rhythmic beats. With the drum kit in place, jazz drummers such as Gene Krupa, Buddy Rich, Chick Webb, and dozens of others helped make jazz—and jazz drumming—famous throughout the world.

Rocking and Drumming

Jazz was the most dominant form of popular music until the late 1940s, when African American rhythm-and-blues musicians created an entirely new style called rock and roll. Drums were at the heart of the music, but the rock beat was simple and straightforward. Rock drummers in the 1950s only needed simple drum kits consisting of a snare, a hi-hat, a cymbal, and a bass drum.

The White Stripes perform in New York City in 2007. Using only guitars and drums, the band achieves a minimalist, twenty-first-century sound.

In the 1960s rock became more sophisticated, and kits expanded with the length and complexity of the songs. Bands such as Cream, Led Zeppelin, and Santana featured extended drum solos during their concerts. The Grateful Dead was the first major rock band to use two drummers—Mickey Hart and Bill Kreutzmann—and between them they loaded up the concert stage each night with dozens of percussive instruments, including gongs, chimes, shakers, rattles, and drums from Africa, India, Cuba, China, Brazil, and elsewhere.

By the twenty-first century, a musical trend of stripped-down simplicity emerged. Several popular groups dispensed with the keyboard, bass, and other instruments to perform with only drums and a single guitar. The White Stripes led the move toward rhythm minimalism. Drummer Meg White played a small drum kit with primal fury backed only by guitarist Jack White. In the 2010s the Black Keys, another guitar-drum duo, rose to the top of the charts driven by the raw rock thunder of drummer Pat Carney.

The "Spirit Side of the Drum"

Whether the sound comes from a huge drum kit or an old gong cast in the tenth century, percussive instruments have bent and shaped the sound of music since humans first walked the earth. From the spiritual beat to the physical dance, every society has had a special place for percussion. As Hart writes:

> You might say drums have two voices. One is technical, having to do with the drum's shape, the material it's made of, its cultural context, and the standard way it's played. Technique gives you this voice—the drum's sweet spot. . . . But once you do, the potential arises for contacting the drum's second voice—one I have come to think of as the spirit side of the drum.[16]

CHAPTER 2

Woodwinds

The deep, pounding rhythm of the drum and the lilting, melodious sound of the flute inhabit opposite ends of the musical spectrum. Both instruments, however, have similar roots in the distant past and have been used by cultures all over the world for religious, martial, and musical purposes.

The flute is the oldest member of the woodwind family, which includes the recorder, clarinet, oboe, bassoon, and saxophone. Woodwinds are so called because they were originally made from wood, although today some woodwinds, such as the flute, are made from silver, and the saxophone is made from brass.

Woodwinds are classified as aerophones because they produce sound when a player blows air into them. The air makes a tone because it is split by the sharp edge of the mouthpiece on a flute, by one reed on a clarinet and saxophone, and by two reeds on an oboe and bassoon. The reed is made from a small piece of reed cane fixed to the mouthpiece of the instrument.

While percussion instruments are struck, and string instruments are plucked or bowed, woodwinds produce sound when a column of air vibrates in the hollow body of the instrument. Musical pitch is determined by how many holes in the instrument are covered by fingers or mechanical keys. The more holes that are covered, the longer the tube of the instrument and the lower the note. It takes practice and skill to coordinate the fingers and lips so that sounds emanate from the woodwind, but many musicians believe the resulting music is worth the effort.

The Ancient Flute

Prehistoric wind instruments were whistles and flutes made from natural materials such as animal bone, shell, wood, or stone. These materials neded to be drilled and shaped into musical instruments, but as flautist and author Raymond Meylan writes, "The means of producing sound have remained virtually unchanged to this day. Nothing essentially new has appeared since antiquity, which suggests that the most important discoveries in this area were made in prehistoric times."[17]

Music historians believe that bone whistles dating back about ten thousand years are some of the oldest flutes ever made. These instruments, found in Europe, China, South America, India, and Mesopotamia, were made from the toe bones of small animals and had single holes drilled through them. For example, ancient bone whistles found in caves

An Egyptian painted relief from around 2400 B.C. shows a man playing an oblique flute, which is played to the side.

in Switzerland were made from the toes of reindeer and small rodents known as voles. These whistles produce extremely high notes barely audible to the human ear, leading researchers to believe that hunters originally used them as animal calls.

Around 3000 B.C., people living in Mesopotamia and Egypt played vertical flutes called nay. These were simply reed tubes that were cut into short lengths. The player held the tube below the lower lip and blew onto the edge, like blowing over the top of a bottle. The shorter the tube, the higher the pitch.

Another primitive woodwind is the oblique flute, a tube about 5 feet (1.5m) in length held to the side and behind the musician's body, and played with the head turned. Ancient Egyptian paintings show people playing the oblique flute. This instrument is still found in Indonesia, Iran, South America, and the Balkan countries, where it is known as a kaval. The bright, cutting tone of the kaval resembles the song of an excited bird flitting through the trees. Silver flutes, such as those used in modern symphony orchestras are based on the oblique flute design, though they are shorter in length. Known as transverse flutes, because the blown air passes across the mouthpiece, or embouchure, the instrument is held parallel to the ground, at a right angle to the player's face. The finger holes or keys in the flute are opened or closed to regulate the amount of air passing through the instrument's body and thus the note being played.

Europe Embraces the Flute

The transverse flute, made from boxwood, was first depicted around the twelfth century in hand-painted books found in French and German monasteries. The instruments remained rather obscure until 1599, when English composer Thomas Morley wrote the first Western music for flutes. This was also the first music written for broken consorts, groupings of several instruments rather than the same instrument of different musical ranges.

By the seventeenth century, flute music was embraced by

the French nobility, a group that set the fashion trends for the rest of Europe, and the instrument gained widespread popularity. The renowned Irish flautist James Galway explains why the flute was adopted by European orchestras:

> [The] flute has a range of interesting, attractive colours, powerful dynamics, and a compass extending from an ominous hollow sound at the bottom to a fierce cutting edge at the top. . . . [The] flute is capable of great expressiveness, but—and here comes the crunch—its expressiveness depends entirely on the skill of the player. . . . With the help of a skilled player or two, the flute's wider resources and greater expressiveness . . . won it acceptance as an orchestral and solo instrument.[18]

Despite its popularity, the old-style wooden flute was problematic for composers because changes in weather could affect the pitch of the instrument, and the instrument was often out of tune with the rest of the orchestra. In addition, flautists often had difficulty pressing their fingers completely over the instrument's tone-holes to achieve certain notes. In 1776 Sir John Hawkins, author of the first history of music in English, wrote about the off-key intonation of the flute: "The . . . flute still retains some degree of [praise] among gentlemen whose ears are not nice enough to inform them that it is never in tune."[19] In 1809 Ludwig van Beethoven put it more candidly, writing to a friend, "I cannot make up my mind to write for the flute because this instrument is too limited and imperfect."[20]

The Boehm Flute

In 1828 the German inventor, musician, and flute maker Theobald Boehm set out to create a flute with better intonation. As Meylan writes, every aspect of the flute "was called into question—profile, material and thickness of the body, the number, size and spacing of the tone-holes, and the size of the embouchure hole."[21] Boehm created a flute with a system of rods, levers, and keys that could be manipulated by the player. This allowed flautists to use a single finger to press a key, which would precisely cover one or more holes. This leap forward in flute design provided a more consistent sound and increased the instrument's musical range.

In 1846 Boehm changed the sound of music once again when his company introduced the solid silver flute. As Boehm describes it:

The superior excellence in regard to tone and intonation of my flute, made entirely of silver . . . was so striking that it was remarked by every one immediately. . . . And even temperature affects them less than wooden flutes, because the metal, being an excellent conductor of heat, reaches its highest possible temperature in a few seconds, so that the pitch cannot rise any higher. . . . The silver flute is preferable for playing in very large rooms because of its . . . unsurpassed brilliancy and [resonance] of its tone.[22]

While silver flutes became very popular among professionals and students alike, wooden flutes have remained in use throughout the years. Made from cocus wood from the West Indies and South America, wooden flutes deliver a dense, warm, rich sound, while those made of silver, platinum, or even gold yield a lighter, lilting sound.

Reeds and Woodwinds

Flute players split the air blown from their lips over the mouthpiece of their instrument. While difficult, the embouchure remains solid and predictable. Players of other woodwinds, however, must split the air by blowing it over a reed, which can have a positive or negative effect on the sound of the instrument. Reed instruments are notoriously finicky and difficult to play. British instrument scholar Anthony Baines explains:

Oboists, clarinetists, and bassoonists are entirely dependent upon a short-lived vegetable matter of merciless capriciousness, with which, however, when it behaves, are wrought perhaps the most tender and expressive sounds of all wind music. . . . No string player has one-tenth the trouble with his sheep's guts [strings] that the reed player has with his bits of a

Mediterranean weed. For in terms of plant economy, this is all that reed cane is.[23]

Reed cane is grown in many places including Italy, Spain, and Mexico, but the finest comes from the area around Cannes, France. The process of making reeds is not automated, and artisans who specialize in making them are rare. As such, many skilled players split, cut, and shape their own reeds, hoping to obtain that elusive and sublime sound. Whatever difficulties a reed player may encounter, musicians who play the oboe have twice as much trouble, because it is an instrument that has two reeds.

The woodwind section of the Vienna Philharmonic Orchestra performs in 1975. Clarinets, bassoons, oboes, and flutes are among the instruments in the woodwind family.

Roots of the Oboe

Oboes are long tubular instruments that resemble clarinets. They are made of dark tropical wood called grenadilla. Modern oboes have fifteen or more silver- or nickel-plated keys. The two reeds protrude from the mouthpiece, and the player produces sounds by blowing over them, causing a column of air to vibrate within the conical bore of the instrument. By manipulating the keys, the player can produce notes in more than three octaves.

The oldest double-reed woodwind ever discovered was found near Ur, Mesopotamia, and is believed to have been made around 2800 B.C. In later centuries, oboe-like instruments became common throughout the Middle East and Africa. Murals of young women playing these instruments were painted in the tombs of ancient Egyptian pharaohs around 1400 B.C.

In the fifth century B.C. the Greeks called their version of the double-reed woodwind the aulos. Its invention was credited to Athena, the goddess of wisdom. The aulos is still played today and has an exotic tone that sounds like a cross between a flute and a violin. In 490 B.C. Greek musician and poet Pindar described the sound of the aulos as "many voiced . . . [and imitates] a cry exceedingly shrill . . . that tune, which oft swelleth forth from the thin plate of brass, and from the reeds which grow beside the fair city of Graces."[24]

The aulos was also used for military purposes. Greek author Thucydides describes Spartan aulos players in battle: "The [Spartans] moved slowly and to the music of many aulos-players, who were stationed in their ranks, and played, not as an act of religion, but in order that the army might march evenly in a true measure, and that the line might not break."[25]

The Romans called the aulos the tibia and made the instruments from metal, bone, and wood. They used tibia players at gladiator games—and after the contests—at funerals. In modern times, updated versions of the ancient aulos are found throughout Asia and the Middle East. In India, players of the shahnai, which resembles the aulos, may play two of the instruments at the same time. An oboe-like instrument known as the hichiriki remains popular in the imperial court of Japan.

Europe's Influence on Woodwinds

Oboe-like woodwinds traveled the same route to Europe as drums and other musical instruments; they were brought

Bagpipes

The bagpipe, most famously played by Scottish Highlanders, is an ancient instrument whose use has been widespread throughout Europe. The instrument consists of an airtight leather bag, which is often covered with cloth. A long melody pipe, or chanter, is fitted with a reed and contains finger holes on which melodies are played. Two other pipes, the tenor drone and bass drone, are also fitted with reeds. Finally, a fourth pipe, or blowpipe, is placed in the player's mouth so that he or she may inflate the bag with air. This is equipped with a one-way valve so air may be blown into the bag but cannot escape into the player's mouth.

A musician holds the bag under his or her left arm and inflates the bag through the blowpipe. As the bag is squeezed under the arm, the air within continually blows over the reeds in the melody and drone pipes, making music even when the musician takes breaths of air. Meanwhile the fingers of both hands open and close the holes on the melody pipe, producing a song, while the drone pipes hum in constant single notes. This action produces loud music that can sometimes carry for miles. As such, the bagpipes have been used on battlefields for centuries.

by Arab traders in the first millennium A.D. The instrument was adopted by wandering minstrels, known as pipers, who also carried guitars, harps, and other small instruments. These minstrels played music for wealthy citizens wherever they went—even into the bath—and piped for the rich on journeys, at banquets, at church services, and before battles. The pipers played several kinds of double-reed oboe-like instruments that were known as shawms in England and pommers in Germany. While the instruments may have been common, according to Baines, their sound was less than enchanting: "[Of] all musical sounds that . . . day to day smote the ears of a sixteenth-century town resident, the deafening skirl [shriek] of the shawm band in palace

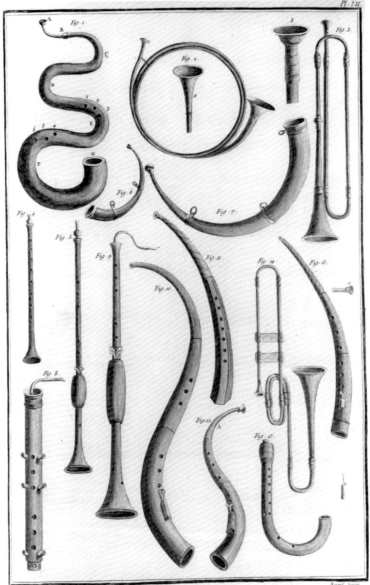

Lutherie, Instrumens anciens, modernes, Etrangers, 'a vent, 'a boat et 'a anche.

courtyard or market square must have been the most famil-iar, save perhaps only for the throbbing of a lute through somebody's open window."[26]

Like the primitive flute, shawms and pommers were not agile enough—or suitably in tune—to play the multipart, or polyphonic, music that emerged during the Renaissance. By the seventeenth century, woodwinds had fallen out of fashion, replaced by the violin and the relatively new brass trumpet. In seventeenth-century France, however, the shawm, known as the hautbois, received a makeover by a woodwind company owned by Jean Hotteterre. The new oboe was divided into three parts—the top, bottom, and bell—and the double reed was placed directly between the lips. The redesigned instrument quickly achieved widespread respect, as Baines writes:

> [The instrument builders] set about designing an improvement on [the shawm] according to their own ideas; a new hautbois that would be altogether more useful in the kinds of music coming into fashion. It would be flexible in dynamic range, and would possess a really good upper register—a register that had previously been badly neglected in reed instruments, but was now urgently required by the new musical styles. . . . From the first the oboe was a success, and as it quickly became known in other countries it seems to have impressed musicians above all through the splendid expressive range of its sound. To the trumpet were allotted airs of joyous and brilliant character; to the flutes, those of the "languishing and melancholy" kind; but the new oboe, like the human voice and the violin, could encompass every mood. In the matter of volume alone, it could be played nearly as loud as a trumpet and yet as soft as the recorder.[27]

Hotteterre's oboe was quickly picked up by musicians in royal courts across [Europe]. King Louis XIV adapted it for military music where three oboes—tenor, bass, and middle—played harmonious parts along with side drums.

By the nineteenth century, composers were writing extremely complex oboe parts that required accuracy and agility not typically found in the instrument. In order to improve its playability and reliability, the Triebert company in Paris remade the oboe. Designers studied Boehm's flutes and devised a method for attaching fifteen silver keys to the oboe. This expanded the musical range of the instrument while making it easier to play.

By the early twentieth century, there were several different key configurations for the oboe; for example, the Viennese oboe is made with thirteen keys, the Floth oboe has eight keys, and the Full Conservatory oboe, used by professionals, has a complex system with twenty-four keys. It was clear that the oboe had evolved from its roots in ancient Egypt into a versatile instrument with a great range and beautiful tone.

The Bassoon

Just as the oboe was derived from the shawm, instruments such as the bass pommer evolved into the bassoon, which is essentially a double-reed bass oboe. The wooden body of the bassoon is made from ebony or boxwood and is divided into four parts—the wing, butt, long joint, and bell joint. The double-reed mouthpiece is attached to the body by a thin, curved metal pipe.

The bassoon has a range that is more than an octave lower than the oboe. (An octave is an eight-note interval between two notes of the same name, such as middle C and tenor C. The higher note vibrates at twice the rate of the lower note.) Like the oboe, there are several types of bassoons that play in various ranges. For example, the contrabassoon, or double bassoon, plays an octave below the bassoon, around the same notes as the lowest keys of a piano. The tenoroon, or tenor bassoon, is a rare instrument smaller than the regular bassoon, which plays in a higher range.

The earliest bassoon-like instruments were found in Germany in the mid-1500s and later throughout Europe. Baines describes the sound:

> With a suitably-made reed, the old "horse's leg," as people called the bassoon in England, sounds irresistibly sweet and beautiful . . . rather cello-like. Like the old oboe, it blends supremely well with every other instrument, while yet it possessed sufficient weight to have been a favorite solo instrument.[28]

Like other woodwinds, instrument makers in France, Germany, and elsewhere tinkered with the bassoon over the centuries, changing the materials, key arrangements, and adding mechanical keys. Since that time, the bassoon has changed little and, like the oboe, remains today as it was perfected in the 1800s.

The Clarinet

While the bassoon is limited to bass parts, the single-reed clarinet is one of the most diverse woodwind instruments, with a range of nearly four octaves. According to British clarinetist Jack Brymer, the clarinet has "a subtler variety of tone quality, from velvet-soft to steely-hard—and . . . [an] ability to blend with other instruments which makes it the essential 'binding' factor of the woodwind section."[29]

Unlike the oboe and bassoon, which evolved over time, the clarinet was created around 1700 by Johann Christoph Denner, a Nuremberg instrument-maker. Denner based his instrument on the primitive chalumeau, a small woodwind that plays high, wavering notes and sounds like a toy trumpet. Denner fashioned a reed mouthpiece for the chalumeau and added several keys to give the instrument a range of more than two octaves. Denner called his invention the clarinette.

Musicians quickly came to appreciate the versatility of the clarinet, and it was popular throughout Europe. The instrument was described by Italian musician Filippo Bonanni in 1722:

> An instrument similar to the oboe is the [clarinet]. It is two and a half palms long and terminates in a bell like the trumpet three inches in width. It is pierced with seven holes in front and one behind. There are in addition two other holes opposite to each other, but not diametrically, which are closed and opened by two springs pressed by the finger.[30]

Composers from Wolfgang Amadeus Mozart to Richard Wagner began composing music for the clarinet, and it was soon found in every symphony orchestra. The sound of the instrument was described in the nineteenth century by author William Gardiner:

> [The clarinet] approaches the tone of the female voice nearer than any other instrument, and as a principal in the orchestra it now sustains a distinguished part. . . .
> In quality of tone it is warm and powerful; partaking

Film director Woody Allen plays clarinet with his New Orleans jazz band in 2007. By the early twentieth century, the clarinet had a strong presence in jazz music.

somewhat of the oboe and the trumpet combined, and the lustre of its tones adds great [radiance] to the orchestra.[31]

Like other woodwinds of the time, the clarinet had a limited range, was not musically accurate, and was difficult to play. This changed when the Boehm mechanical key system was added to the clarinet in 1843. By this time, the clarinet was made from African Blackwood. The material earned the clarinet the name "licorice stick" when it became an integral part of New Orleans jazz music at the turn of the twentieth century.

The Saxophone

The last woodwind to be invented was conceived in 1841 by Belgian inventor Adolphe Sax, who named the instrument after himself. The brass saxophone, or "the sound of Sax," is classified as a woodwind because it is played with a reed.

Sax developed at least fourteen different horns for the saxophone family, varying in size and key. They included the E-flat soprano, B-flat soprano, F alto, C tenor, E-flat baritone, C bass, and E-flat contrabass. Today the fourteen horns of Sax have been reduced to four standard sizes that remain in widespread use: the alto, tenor, soprano, and baritone.

The most popular type of saxophone, the alto, features a ninety-degree bend after the mouthpiece and then doubles back on itself after a two-and-one-half-foot section with twenty keys. There is a flared bell at the end. The alto is smaller, but similar in shape to the tenor. The soprano saxophone is straight and resembles a brass clarinet. The baritone saxophone is the largest and lowest-pitched instrument.

The Jazz Clarinet

While woodwinds remained part of symphony orchestras, the clarinet took on a life of its own in twentieth-century jazz bands. The use of the clarinet in jazz music is explored by music professor John Robert Brown:

Listen to almost any performance from the first decade of recorded jazz and you will hear the sound of the clarinet. Whether you choose to listen to the Original Dixieland Jazz Band . . . the King Oliver/Louis Armstrong recordings or Jelly Roll Morton's Red Hot Peppers, you will hear every ensemble topped by upper-register clarinet, playing in harmony above the melody.

All the evidence about the origins of jazz points to the music having developed from vocal performances. After the end of the Civil War in 1865 the New Orleans blacks were able gradually to acquire the instruments of the military band, including the clarinet. Military (marching) bands were important in all-French settlements, and in New Orleans most of the early jazz players started their careers in such wind bands, playing marches, polkas, quadrilles and so on. From these two sources—the vocal folk/dance music and the marching band—it is quite easy to understand how the five- or six-piece jazz bands evolved. . . . [And] it is with these smaller "marching bands," with their trumpet-trombone-clarinet front line, that jazz first appeared. . . . [During the swing era] in the late 1930s . . . jazz became the pop music of the day; [it was] the age of the big swing band fronted and led by a virtuoso instrumentalist. This was the heyday of [clarinetist] Benny Goodman, the "King of Swing," and Artie Shaw, the "King of the Clarinet." . . . Goodman made his first trio recordings when he was not yet eighteen . . . [and] is the clarinettist's clarinettist.

Quoted in Colin Lawson, ed. *The Cambridge Companion to the Clarinet.* Cambridge, England: Cambridge University Press, 1995, p. 184.

When it was first introduced by Sax, the sound of the saxophone seemed remarkable to musicians. Upon first hearing the instrument, the Italian composer Gioachino Rossini proclaimed, "This is the most beautiful kind of sound that I have ever heard!"[32]

The new horn gained widespread publicity in 1845 when Sax proposed a "battle of the bands" to show the superiority of his instruments before an audience of twenty thousand in Paris. The battle was between a band of forty-five musicians playing traditional instruments and a similar-sized band made up entirely of saxophonists. Author J.G. Kastner, who attended the battle of the bands, described the contest:

> Sax's large infantry band of saxhorns . . . compared favourably with the older [-style traditional orchestra], which suffered . . . from the enormous gap in the middle harmonies, the thin cutting tone of the oboes mixing ill with the rest, the swollen-faced bassoonists with no carrying power whatever, and despite some good use of valve horns, the sterile buzzing of hand-horns in the open air, still worse on the march.[33]

The general opinion was that the saxophones blew away the competition, and the instruments' inventor was awarded a contract to supply the French military with saxophones. During the following decades, several major composers wrote works utilizing the saxophone. Georges Bizet's opera *L'Arlésienne* and Maurice Ravel's famous orchestral work *Bolero* were among the most notable compositions. By the end of the twentieth century, an estimated two thousand ballets, operas, and symphonies included saxophone parts.

Soulful Sounds

Meanwhile, at the turn of the century, the influence of French marching bands was strong in New Orleans when African American musicians combined military music with ragtime and blues to create a new musical style called jazz. While early jazz horn players used cornets, trombones, tubas, and clarinets, by the 1920s clarinetists, who were skilled at playing a single-reed instrument, began adding the saxophone to their repertoires.

Saxophones of Rock and Soul

Though mainly associated with jazz, saxophones were part of the rock-and-roll revolution in the 1950s and 1960s, as Richard Ingham and John Helliwell write in The Cambridge Companion to the Saxophone:

Saxophone solos in the Bill Haley band were taken by tenor player Rudy Pompelli (*Shake, Rattle and Roll*, 1954), and despite the growing domination of the (electric) guitar, the saxophone was relied on to push the excitement factor in many bands. Lee Allen featured with Little Richard and Fats Domino, King Curtis was the soloist on the Coasters' *Yakety Yak* (1958) and *Charlie Brown* (1959), and Ray Charles used Hank Crawford for many years. . . . The early 1960s produced two novelty numbers which were none the less influential in their own way, Boots Randolph's *Yakety Sax* (1963) and Henry Mancini's classic *Pink Panther* . . . in 1964. The decade as a whole produced the great solo artistry of King Curtis and Junior Walker on the one hand, and the soul horn sections of James Brown and the Motown groups on the other. Junior Walker and King Curtis, both tenor players, were enormously influential and enjoyed great commercial success. They de-fined the rock tenor sound of the 1960s, with extraordinary control of high tones, flutter-tonguing, growls, shakes and, above all, sensitive phrasing. . . . Walker was a singer as well as a saxophonist—his hits included *Shotgun* (1965) and *How Sweet It Is* (1966). . . . The horn section developed in this decade into a regular feature, particularly with the Motown vocal groups. . . . The horns were a vital part of the James Brown sound, from *Out of Sight* (1964), the beginnings of funk, through *Cold Sweat* (1967) and into the 1970s. The end of the 1960s saw jazz embracing rock in the work of Miles Davis and others; in the band Blood, Sweat and Tears . . . known as a rock "big band," one of [its] most notable recordings was *Spinning Wheel*. . . . The successful band Chicago included Walter Parazaider on saxophone. These groundbreaking ventures also seemed to give legitimacy to the idea of jazz artists being used as session players for rock and pop recordings.

Richard Ingham and John Helliwell. *The Cambridge Companion to the Saxophone.* Cambridge, England: Cambridge University Press, 1998, p. 154.

Louis Jordan—seen performing with his band around 1970—developed the "jump blues" sound in the 1940s. His music was a major influence on what would become rock and roll.

The saxophone was perfect for improvising jazz music, because it could express the guttural honk of the low-down blues, the smoky melancholy of slow dance music, and the soaring riffs of melodious swing tunes. By the 1930s big band composers such as Duke Ellington were filling their orchestras with five saxophone players—two altos, two tenors, and a baritone.

Louis Jordan, who sang, composed, and played the alto sax, developed the fast-paced jump blues sound, writing songs in the 1940s such as "Caldonia," "Ain't Nobody Here But Us Chickens," and "Choo Choo Ch'Boogie" that were the forerunners of rock and roll. During the fifties, players such as alto sax wizard Charlie Parker revolutionized jazz and the way the saxophone was played. Parker specialized in bebop—manic music with complex harmonies and melodies. In the sixties, saxophonist John Coltrane went beyond bebop to play free-form jazz, wringing improvised sounds from the saxophone that no one had previously believed were humanly possible.

The Sound of Breath

Woodwind instruments have played an important role in classical music since the Middle Ages. Most symphony orchestras employ four flutes, four oboes, and a pair of bassoons. After the invention of the clarinet, orchestras used four clarinetists as well. While most orchestras do not have specific saxophone sections, clarinetists sometimes double as sax players.

The music of the woodwinds can be described as organic, adding the music of nature—and human breath—to the orchestra. Galway sums up this feeling in the following passage written about the flute:

> The sound comes from inside the body, in a way not possible with instruments to be hit or scraped. It is an extension of the player's speaking and singing voice. His breath, his muscles, his fingers produce the sound, without intervening technical complications. Nothing separates him from the tone, no mechanism . . . no hammer, no bow nor string. Only singers have less paraphernalia between them and their listeners.[34]

CHAPTER 3

Brass

I n the era before microphones and amplifiers, brass instruments created the loudest sounds emanating from any orchestra. Their attention-attracting reverberations were used by kings in their royal courts and were essential to generals on the battlefield.

Even today, few unamplified instruments can surpass the volume, brightness, and resonance of a well-played trumpet, tuba, or trombone. Whether performing a delicate passage written by Ludwig van Beethoven or marching across a football field blaring "Louie Louie," brass sections hold a unique place in musical history and have been used in nearly every style of music from classical to rock and roll. As trombonist and music professor Trevor Herbert writes, "There is probably no other family of instruments which has been more affected by the progress of history, with its attendant social changes, technical inventions and musical fashions."[35]

Vibrating Sound Waves

Like woodwinds, brass instruments such as trumpets, tubas, and French horns are aerophones, but differ from flutes, oboes, and clarinets in how they are played. Instead of a column of air vibrating within the instrument, as happens

with woodwinds, brass instruments amplify the vibrations caused by the musician's lips.

This process is explained by instrument researcher Arnold Myers:

> The column of air inside the tube is set into vibration when it is excited by the player buzzing his/her lips placed against the mouthpiece. A sustained sound on brass instruments requires . . . sound waves travelling from one end to the other and reflected from each end like water waves in a bath. . . . Whether the other end of the instrument terminates abruptly (as in a bugle) or terminates with a flaring bell (as in a trumpet), sound waves are reflected by the bell mouth or by the flare.[36]

Musicians create sound from brass instruments by blowing air into a mouthpiece. When the air within the brass tube starts vibrating, the tiny particles form fast-moving wave patterns that vibrate back and forth. By blowing harder or softer, the player can change the wave pattern to produce different notes. For example, by blowing with relaxed lips, a trumpet player can play the lowest note on

Trombone players play during Carnival in Oruro, Bolivia. Brass instruments have been incorporated into cultural events and traditions around the world.

Making Brass Instruments

Brass is an alloy metal composed of about 70 percent copper and 30 percent zinc. The natural trumpet of the Renaissance era was made from fourteen separate pieces of brass. The bell, tubing, saddles, and other pieces were made from sheet brass that was wrapped into various shaped tubes. The seams were then sealed with an alloy solder. The brass, however, often became hard and brittle when it was bent, hammered, and stretched. To keep the metal soft, it had to be heated to a red-hot temperature and then cooled. This blackened the surface of the metal with an oxide layer that later had to be removed by what was known as "pickling" in a bath of acid.

Before this was done, however, the bell was formed by heating, cooling, and hammering. Finally the instrument was burnished, or finely shaped, on a metal rod called a mandrel, sanded, and polished to a fine finish.

Machinery has taken over much of the work of making modern brass instruments. The sheet metal is cut and formed by machines, which are run by highly skilled workers. The bell is formed on an electric lathe that spins the metal at a high speed while it is shaped by a worker using wooden shaping wands, knives, and other tools.

To bend the tubing, liquid lead is poured into the tube and allowed to cool. The tube may then be bent by hand without collapsing or cracking. Once it is finished, the tube is heated and the lead is poured out. Cheaper instruments are bent by machines.

The bell is soldered to the tubing, and more than 150 parts come together to make a modern instrument such as a trumpet. Valves must be made with space-age accuracy, with the pistons that move up and down inside the mechanism set at no more than one ten-thousandth of an inch from the valve wall.

his instrument—called the fundamental note. By tightening the lips and blowing harder, the player may produce a sound one octave—or eight notes—higher than the fundamental note. This is called the first overtone. By blowing harder still—and with tighter lips—the player produces a pitch that is one octave plus five notes higher, called the second overtone. This process can be completed to produce what is known as an overtone series.

The overtones emanating from the instrument may be changed by valves moved up and down by the fingers, as in a trumpet, tuba, or French horn. On a trombone, overtones are changed as the player moves the slide back and forth to change the length of the air column. Bugles do not have valves, so players can play the notes in the overtone series, but not scales or melodies. As such, bugle players can play only five notes. They perform simple songs such as "Taps" or "Reveille" by changing the vibrations of their lips to change pitch.

The Historical Trumpet

Musicologists believe that the first trumpet may have been a tree branch made hollow by rot or insects. Unlike modern trumpets, these ancient instruments had no mouthpiece and no flared bell. They were not even used to make music, but were instead used as megaphones to amplify a person's voice so that it could be heard at great distances. Shamans used this distorted noise to gain the attention of the gods or to ward off evil spirits, as trumpeter and musicologist Edward Tarr explains:

> Such megaphone trumpets were sounded at religious and magical rites: circumcisions, burials and sunset ceremonies. They were played only by men and were thus identified with the male sex, as opposed to certain drum forms which were supposed to be feminine. Trumpets such as these can still be found in the primitive cultures of New Guinea and northwest Brazil, as well as in the form of the Australian didjeridu.[37]

Later trumpets with a more refined sound may have been made from conch shells, animal horns, elephant tusks, and even human thighbones.

In ancient Egypt, trumpets, like many other musical instruments, were used for military and religious purposes. More than four thousand years ago, the ancient Egyptians believed that trumpets were invented by Osiris, the god of the underworld. The trumpets, about 20 inches (51cm) long, were played during military and religious ceremonies. The instruments did not make enjoyable music according to the Greek historian Plutarch, who wrote, "the blare of an Egyptian trumpet was like [a donkey's] bray."[38] Despite such

Indian and Asian Trumpets

Trumpeter and musicologist Edward Tarr describes trumpets native to India and Tibet:

The South Indian trumpet, called *tirucinnam* in Tamil, was similar to the . . . Egyptian trumpet. It was about [30 inches (76.2cm)] long, had a wide cylindrical bore, and a narrow, conical bell, but no mouthpiece. The reason for the lack of mouthpiece is clear; the tirucinnam player always blew two of these instruments simultaneously.

Another kind of Indian trumpet, the end-blown shell trumpet called *sankha* in Sanskrit is mentioned here only because of its exclusively religious use. On the last day of the earth, when everything goes up in flames, the god Siva will play the shell trumpet—as will the seven angels of the biblical Last Judgment.

The modern North Indian trumpet seems to be derived from central Asiatic and Far Eastern trumpets or at least to be related to them. Like the Chinese trumpet, it is narrow and conical and consists of four telescoping sections, the ends of which are each provided with a kind of knob. Besides the end-blown shell trumpet (hai lo in Chinese, hora in Japanese), which is played by sailors and Buddhist priests, there was also in China a very long cylindrical metal trumpet (hao t'ung in Chinese, dokaku in Japanese), the bell end of which rests on the ground while the instrument is being played. . . . The hao t'ung was played at burials. . . .

The Tibetan trumpet, called *dung*, can be as long as nearly [16 feet (4.8m) in length]. It is made of copper, has a conical bore, and also consists of several telescoping sections with knobs. When it is blown during lama rites, it usually rests on the ground. Like many Asiatic trumpet instruments related to it, the dung has a broad, very flat mouthpiece. Only low, roaring tones are played on it.

Edward Tarr. *The Trumpet.* London: B.T. Batsford, 1988, pp. 30–31.

criticism, Egyptian trumpets were made from hammered silver or bronze, extremely valuable, and only possessed by the richest, most powerful people.

Trumpets made from silver are also mentioned prominently in the Bible. In the Book of Numbers, God tells

Moses, "And when you go to war in your land against the adversary who oppresses you, then you shall sound the alarm with trumpets . . . and you should be saved from your enemies. On the day after gladness also, and reported feasts, at the beginnings of your months, you should blow the trumpets." The ancient Israelites also used a trumpet made from a ram's horn called a shofar, which is still blown on Jewish holidays.

The ancient Greek trumpet, known as the salpinx, was made from straight tubing more than 5 feet (1.5m) long, had more than a dozen sections made of ivory, and was held together with bronze rings. The mouthpiece and flared end, or bell, were made from cast bronze, and the tone was described by one ancient poet as "screaming."[39]

The Romans called their trumpet a tuba, although it little resembled a modern tuba. Used by soldiers on the march, this instrument was about 4 feet (1.2m) long and made from a straight tube with a bell on the end. The Romans also had a type of trumpet known as a lituus, a J-shaped shrieking instrument used to frighten the enemy in war.

Angels herald the Last Judgment by sounding trumpets in this sixteenth-century fresco by Michelangelo in the Vatican's Sistine Chapel. Trumpets have been used in religious and spiritual ceremonies of various cultures throughout history.

Improving the Trumpet

By the Middle Ages (A.D. 400–1500), trumpets were widely used across Europe. At that time, kings, princes, knights, and other nobility employed wandering minstrels who played 2- to 6-foot-long trumpets (0.6 to 1.8m) at coronations, weddings, banquets, jousting matches, ceremonies, and festivals. Trumpeters playing on long horns announced the arrival of aristocrats at public events. German soldiers in guard towers used thurmers, or tower trumpets, to blare a warning when enemies were approaching.

By this time, the nearly universal word for the instrument was found in several European languages. To the French it was the trompe, or trompette; in German, trumpa or trompete; in English, trumpet. The English also referred to trumpet-like instruments as claro or clarion, meaning "bright" or "clear," words that help explain the sound of the instruments.

The European trumpets were improved by new innovations in metalwork, as brass instrument expert Keith Polk explains:

> [Instruments] were available fabricated in "S" shapes by the late fourteenth century, and in the standard "folded" form by shortly after 1400. Once the bent forms were developed they soon took over. Straight instruments continued to be made but for most purposes players prefer the portability and control afforded by the new shapes.[40]

These folded, or natural, trumpets were about 3½ feet long, made with tubing about ½ inch (1.2cm) wide, and held a 4-inch (10cm) bell at one end. They were pitched to play either in the key of C or D and could play very high notes.

The improved accuracy of metalworking also allowed for the development of a new kind of instrument, the slide trumpet. This instrument was composed of a mouthpiece and a straight tube about 1 foot (30cm) long, over which another foot-long tube with a bell slid back and forth. When the bell piece was slid out, it lowered the note; when it was pulled toward the player, it shortened the tube, thus raising the note.

The slide trumpet was often played in bands called alta ensembles with other loud instruments such as shawms.

These groups were extremely popular in Italy, Spain, and Portugal.

The Musical Trumpet

By the late fifteenth century, the Renaissance was changing art and music across Europe. Alta ensembles with several styles of trumpet were extremely popular in Italy, Spain, and Portugal. In Germany, the changes even affected tower trumpeters. Besides guarding city walls, groups of tower trumpeters were required to perform together twice daily. According to a sixteenth-century book called *The Tower Players' and Trumpeters' Oath*, trumpeters were expected to "play five entire compositions of proper length, both in the evening . . . and in the morning at daybreak. And this shall be done from both sides of the tower."[41]

These municipal trumpeters played in five-part harmony in which every musician played in a different range. They also performed in orchestras with as many as ten musicians, playing bass, middle, and high parts. These groups not only performed at local dances but also played the most advanced classical music of the day. As Polk writes:

> [Trumpet] players were capable of performing in a variety of [counterpoint] styles, and . . . demands on their memory capacity were considerable. That is, their "unwritten" performances were probably a mixture of improvisations based on secular and sacred . . . melodies, and of repertoires of composed pieces, sacred and secular, in the most demanding styles of the day. . . . Once restricted to the marginal role of ritual, these musicians were now assuming a central role in the art music of their time.[42]

By the eighteenth century, composers such as Johann Sebastian Bach and George Frideric Handel were regularly writing music for the natural trumpet. The part for the highest register was called the clarion; the part beneath it was the second clarion. Below that came the trompa part—about the range of the modern trumpet. The lowest parts were played on a 7-foot-long trumpet known as the principale.

The Ambassador of Jazz

Cornet and trumpet player Louis Armstrong was born in 1901 in a New Orleans, Louisiana, neighborhood so rough it was called "the Battlefield." He went on to become one of the most influential figures in the history of jazz, as critic Alyn Shipton explains:

Like almost all aspiring New Orleans cornetists, Armstrong played in marching bands for parades and funerals. In his late teens he also played in a dance band on the riverboat steamers that went between New Orleans and St. Louis. . . . But from the earliest days, Armstrong's mentor was [cornetist] King Oliver, and when Oliver started his new career in Chicago . . . it was not long before the young Louis traveled north to join Oliver's Creole Jazz Band. . . . Soon, Louis was more famous than his boss. . . . [In 1925] he began to lead his own small groups, the Hot Five and Hot Seven, in record studios. . . . His bands made a series of remarkable discs that include many of the best jazz cornet solos he recorded. Through these, in the space of a few years, he altered the whole course of jazz history by abandoning the idea of group or collective improvisation around a theme. He replaced that approach with a single instrumentalist playing extended solos between choruses by the group, to display both inventive musical ideas and technical prowess. His "West End Blues" and other tracks like "Hotter than That" and "Potato Head Blues" became jazz classics. . . . During the years he led these influential recording bands, he changed from playing cornet to the more incisive trumpet.

Alyn Shipton. *Jazz Makers: Vanguards of Sound.* New York: Oxford University Press, 2002, pp. 26–27.

Jazz icon Louis Armstrong revolutionized jazz by structuring songs around extended solos.

During the classical period of the late eighteenth century, however, composers began to favor the flowing melodies produced by violins and woodwinds. Distraught trumpeters and brass makers, fearing the trumpet might fall out of fashion, began to search for new ways to improve the instrument. In 1818 two musicians, Heinrich Stölzel of the Royal Opera Orchestra of Berlin and Friedrich Blühmel, an amateur oboist, changed the instrument forever when they invented a trumpet with two valves. Valves allowed trumpeters, for the first time, to play the chromatic scale—that is, all notes within its range, including sharps and flats.

The patent for valves was sold to a German instrument company, and soon trumpet players from Russia to England were picking up the valve trumpet. In 1826 a third valve was added. This inspired composers to write new music for the valve trumpet. In 1835 the opera *La Juive* by Jacques Halévy was the first to feature the instrument. Since that time, the valve trumpet has been used in operas, symphony orchestras, Broadway musicals, jazz bands, rock and soul groups, and nearly every other type of musical ensemble.

A Family of Trumpets

Trumpets are made in many different sizes and shapes. Because of the length of the tube in a basic trumpet, the instrument is tuned to play in the key of B-flat. Trumpets that are slightly shorter play in the keys of C, D, E, or even higher. These smaller trumpets are used to play the clarino (high register of the trumpet) parts written by Bach and others. The piccolo trumpet is very small—half the length of the standard B-flat trumpet—and is meant to play an octave higher. On the other end of the musical scale, the bass trumpet—twice as long as the B-flat—plays an octave lower than the standard trumpet.

The cornett is a wooden horn, sort of a cross between a brass and a woodwind instrument, with six keys and a cup mouthpiece. The sound is produced by the player's vibrating lips, but this is modified by holes placed, like a flute, along the length of the instrument.

These instruments were originally made from animal horns more than fifteen centuries ago and are still played in rural areas of Scandinavia where bull or goat horns are used to make primitive cornetts. During the Renaissance, cornetts were very popular because their sound resembled a human voice. As horn player Bruce Dickey writes:

By the mid sixteenth century cornetts appeared in a rich variety of ensembles and settings from cathedrals to princely chambers, from public piazzas to court chapels. Moreover, their popularity spread to every part of Europe, undoubtedly fostered by the performances of virtuosi travelling in the retinues of emperors and princes. . . . Their [the musicians] duties were precisely spelled out: daily performances in the public square, accompanying the entrances and exits of prominent officials as well as providing entertainment for their meals, playing for processions and at public celebrations, etc.[43]

Bugles—short trumpets without valves—also date back to antiquity, and the first ones were probably made from bull horns; in fact, the name bugle comes from an old French word meaning "young bull." Bugles, or bugle-horns, became popular with nobility during the Middle Ages and were used for hunting calls and military signals. With the advent of metalworking technology in the seventeenth century, bugle makers began to form the instruments from copper or brass. At this time they were used by town watchmen, stagecoach drivers, and deliverymen to announce the arrival of the mail. The modern bugle, at around 4 feet (1.5m) in length, took its present form around 1800 and has changed little since then.

Although the bugle has remained the same, around 1830 an anonymous Vienna instrument maker added a valve to the bugle. He called the instrument a flugelhorn after the instrument blown by the Flügelmeister, an official who presided over German hunting expeditions. Shorter and fatter than a regular trumpet, the flugelhorn is about the same length.

Flugelhorns, with their full, sensuous, and subtle tones, are not often used in classical music where the clear, bright sound of the trumpet is preferred. With its rich, dark sound, however, the flugelhorn was adopted by twentieth-century jazz trumpet players such as Chet Baker and, most notably, Miles Davis. In the early 1950s, Davis gave birth to a style called cool jazz, defined by the rich, smoky tone and smooth sound of his flugelhorn.

Like the flugelhorn, the cornet (not to be confused with the cornett) is a type of keyed bugle. It has a softer, less piercing tone than the trumpet. With a bright, brassy tone, cornets were popular in theater, orchestra, and military marching bands in nineteenth-century Europe. Like the flugelhorn, the cornet was adapted by jazz musicians, particularly Louis Armstrong. In the 1920s, Louis Armstrong popularized jazz music throughout the world by improvising hot licks while hitting the highest notes on his cornet.

The Trombone

An instrument that evolved from the trumpet, but is not in the same family, is the trombone, which has a wider—and much lower—range than the B-flat trumpet. The name itself is composed of two Italian words: *trompe*, or "trumpet," and *one*, or "big." In England, it was known by the curious term "sackbut," which is actually based on the German word *sacabuche*, or "draw-pipe."

Trombones have a cup-shaped mouthpiece and a U-shaped slide mechanism. With a narrow bell, the instrument has a mellower tone than a trumpet. Originating from the slide trumpet around 1400, by the 1600s the trombone had evolved into three basic styles: alto, tenor, and bass. Like many other brass instruments, the trombone was favored in eighteenth-century military bands as well as in church and chamber orchestras. Players in modern jazz groups and marching bands prefer the tenor trombone.

The slide allows trombonists to play both individual notes and glissandi, or sliding tones. With the slide pulled in, the trombone plays in a low B-flat key. As the slide is opened, the tube of the instrument is lengthened and the pitch lowers.

Unlike early unvalved trumpets, the trombone could play the entire chromatic scale. As such, composers favored trombones over trumpets and wrote music for them in opera scores. The 1787 opera *Don Giovanni* by Wolfgang Amadeus Mozart features one of the earliest orchestral compositions for trombone. Beethoven's Fifth Symphony is notable for establishing the trombone's place in the symphony orchestra.

The French Horn

The French horn, with its funnel-like mouthpiece, wide, circular tubing, and large flared bell, was developed around the mid-seventeenth century. Its tone has been described as "velvet," meaning that it has a mellower, richer sound than horns in the trumpet family. It was not always this way, however. The French horn was developed around 1650 in France, not surprisingly. At the time it was called the cor de chasse, roughly "horn of the chase," and used to call people from afar while hunting. This blaring horn was considered too raucous to be included in the orchestra with the subtle flutes and violins, and made an appearance on the opera stage only as a special effects instrument.

In Germany and Austria, however, the horn was a favorite of Count Franz Anton von Sporck, who was a music lover as well as an avid hunter. The count ordered several of his musicians to learn the instrument and use it in classical music compositions. By the 1700s, composers began to appreciate the unique sound of the French horn and composed specifically for the instrument. The most colorful parts for the horn were written in the upper, or clarino, range.

By the mid-1700s, musicians developed the hand horn technique for the French horn, in which the player inserted the right hand into the bell. By moving the hand back and forth, players were able to play notes other than the fundamental tone and overtones, thus filling in the previously missing notes in the chromatic scale. By the end of the century, the orchestral horn, as it was now called, became a necessary part of every orchestra. Composers such as Franz Joseph Haydn, Mozart, and Beethoven wrote majestic solo pieces specifically for the orchestral horn.

In the 1830s, the addition of three valves, similar to those used in the trumpet, broadened the range of the instrument further, allowing a standard horn in the key of F to play the

A high school band member plays the French horn at a 2007 parade in Brooklyn, New York. The hand horn technique she uses was developed by musicians in the seventeenth century.

chromatic scale over three octaves. Late in the nineteenth century, an additional valve was added that, when depressed, changed the entire key of the orchestral horn from F to B-flat. This four-valve instrument, known as the double horn, is widely used today—and not only in classical music. In the 1960s the Beatles helped popularize the sound of the French horn in pop music. The instrument may be heard on the 1966 song "For No One" and the title track from the 1967 album *Sgt. Pepper's Lonely Hearts Club Band.*

The Tuba

While the orchestral horn player reaches for the high notes, no brass player hits lower notes than the tuba player. Based on the Latin word for trumpet, the tuba was patented in 1835 by Friedrich Wilhelm Wieprecht, a Prussian bandmaster, and Johann Gottfried Moritz, a German instrument maker. The inventors based their new instrument on the bass bugle with valves and the S-shaped wooden horn called a serpent.

The tuba is the largest of the brass instruments. With a wide-bore, coiled tubing, three to five valves, a deep cuplike mouthpiece, and large, upward bell, the instrument is the deep "oompah" bass of the orchestra or band. While able to cover a three-octave range, the F tuba can reach the second C below middle C.

Tubas come in various pitches, based on the length of the tubing. The most popular tuba, the Bb, has a main tube 18 feet (5.4m) long. The higher-pitched C tuba has 16 feet (4.8m) tubing while the Eb has 13 feet (4m). One of the largest tubas ever made, called a subcontrabass, was created by Bohemian instrument maker Václav Cerveny in 1855. The instrument had 45 feet (13.7m) of tubing and was 8 feet (2.4m) high.

Since the nineteenth century, most orchestras have employed at least one tuba player, and several well-known works were composed to feature the instrument. Richard Wagner asked Moritz to create a smaller tuba with almost no flare in the bell for use in his opera *The Ring of the Nibelung,* which premiered in 1875. Igor Stravinsky used the tuba in his immortal *The Rite of Spring,* written in 1913. The movement "Bydlo" from Modest Mussorgsky's 1874 *Pictures at an Exhibition* is among the most famous tuba solos in classical music.

Early New Orleans jazz musicians were quick to employ the unique bass sounds of the tuba. The thumping rhythm of the instrument helped keep parade marchers in line while adding a raucous element of humor to the music. The tuba played an integral role in jazz music until the 1940s, when string basses took over playing the lowest notes in a band.

The Tuba Revolution

For decades the tuba was rarely seen outside marching bands. That changed in the mid-2000s with the growing popularity of Mexican-style banda dance music in Southern California. Banda groups utilize woodwinds, percussion, trombones, and trumpets, but tubas act as the lead instrument. The sound emerged in Mexico in the late nineteenth century and was long shunned by young people in the United States. That changed in the early twenty-first century as DJ Raul Campos told the *New York Times*, "[The status of] banda has really grown. It's like a new, cool trend with young people. It's now cool to have a live band with a tuba, or to be a tuba player."[44]

The growing fad for banda and tuba players created what some called the tuba revolution. *Los Angeles Times* reporter Sam Quinones explains how the tuba evolved from instrument to status symbol during this time:

> The mania for the instrument arrived from Mexico . . . and is fueled by the large number of house parties that occur [in Los Angeles] every weekend. Immigrants who once were too poor to hold such parties in their homeland now view a tuba-equipped banda as a sign of having arrived. Tuba players say partygoers now throw wadded dollar bills into their instruments— sometimes so many that they clog the pipes.[45]

While tuba players were suddenly finding themselves in great demand, the banda craze was not good for everyone. Demand for the instrument fueled a rash of tuba thefts in Southern California in 2012. Dozens of tubas, some worth several thousand dollars, disappeared from middle schools and high schools, leaving marching bands in the lurch.

The tuba revolution demonstrates that brass instruments have been in great demand since the biblical Gabriel blew his silver horn. From the shrieking blast meant to scare the enemy on a battlefield to the sublime sounds of a modern jazz quartet, brass instruments tell a story in music that is nearly as old as humanity itself.

CHAPTER 4

Strings

Instruments with strings, such as the guitar and violin, are some of the most popular in the world. The family of stringed instruments has been part of human history for tens of thousands of years.

Cave paintings in France dating back nearly fifteen thousand years depict a man with what researchers believe is a one-stringed instrument being played with a bow or possibly being hit with a rhythm stick. This type of primitive instrument was probably made from animal sinew rolled tightly into a string and possibly stretched across a gourd.

Whether a stringed instrument is plucked, struck, strummed, or played with a musical bow, it is called a chordophone. The sound of chordophones is produced by vibrating strings stretched across two fixed points.

Some of the most ancient stringed instruments were simple one-string musical bows that varied little from hunting bows. The strings of primitive music bows were made from tightly rolled animal gut, material commonly found in the intestines of sheep and cows. (Although this type of string material is sometimes referred to as catgut, cats were never used for this purpose.) The string was stretched across a flexible stick 1.5 to 10 feet (0.5 to 3m) in length. A more advanced version of a musical bow might have had a hollow gourd attached to it to give the instrument volume

Some of the most popular modern instruments, such as the violin, banjo, and guitar, belong to the chordophone family.

and resonance. To play the instrument, the string was hit rhythmically with a stick.

By 1900 B.C., ancient Babylonian paintings showed nude figures strumming stringed instruments called lutes, which resembled guitars. Later, in ancient Egypt, people plucked harps and lyres.

The chordophone family has three branches. The first includes instruments with a neck, such as guitars, violins, cellos, banjos, Indian sitars, and mandolins. These have strings of equal length that are of varying thickness and tension. The musician changes the pitch of the strings by pressing down in various places along the neck with the fingers. This action shortens the strings, thus producing higher pitch results. The strings are set into vibration by strumming or plucking with fingers, picks, or bows.

The second branch features instruments such as the zither, dulcimer, and Japanese koto, which utilize strings stretched across a flat body. A third branch includes plucked instruments with multiple strings, such as the lyre, where each string produces only one pitch. Harps are part of this family, which is further divided into two subcategories: the harp proper, in which the strings may be plucked by either hand from each side, and the psaltery, where the strings are stretched over a *soundboard* and may be played only from one side. (A soundboard is a thin sheet of wood placed under—or above—the strings to increase resonance.)

The Ancient Lyre

The lyre, or lyra, is among the oldest instruments classified as a chordophone. These instruments have gut strings (made from sheep intestine) that stretch between a frame, or crossbar, and a soundboard. The crossbar is supported by two arms that are attached to each side of the instrument's body. The strings are attached to the soundboard at the string holder.

The lyre was well known in ancient Greece and was said to be the chief instrument played by Orpheus, the child of the sun god Apollo. At that time lyres were divided by their number of strings. Some lyres were depicted with seven strings or fewer, while others held eight or more. Those with eight or more strings were played by musicians who used both hands to pluck each string separately. Those with seven strings or fewer were played in a style called block and strum, in which the musician strums the strings with either the back of the hand or a pick held between the thumb and fingers. Meanwhile, the right-handed player uses his or her left hand to block, or mute, certain strings so they do not sound.

The ancient Greeks used two basic types of the instrument. Amateurs played the bowl lyre, whose body was made from a turtle shell, wooden bowl, or bull skin. The box lyre—known as the kithara and played by professionals—had hollow, symmetrical arms attached to a hollow wooden boxlike body that was square or rectangular. Kitharas had eight or more strings. They were played by musicians who used both hands to pluck each string separately. According to music historian Frederic V. Grunfeld, for more than one thousand years the kithara "reigned as the chief instrument of the public games and religious festivals of Greece and Rome."[46]

Lyres made from various materials in many shapes and sizes have been found in numerous cultures. African lyres, for example, were mainly round or square and had three to ten strings with bodies made from wood, gourds, or animal parts. In Finland a rectangular lyre with two or three strings and played with a bow was called a jouhikko.

A fresco from a fifth century B.C. tomb in Tarquinia, Italy, shows an Etruscan musician with a lyre.

The Aristocratic Harp

Like the lyre, the harp is an instrument dating back to the days of ancient Babylon and Egypt. The harp was likely derived from the lyre. There are three basic harp shapes: the bowed or arched harp, the angle harp, and the triangle or frame harp that resembles the modern instrument. The harp is played by plucking the strings that run between a sound box and a neck. These strings run at a ninety-degree angle to the sound box instead of parallel, as on a violin.

The bow-shaped harp is the most ancient of instruments and does not resemble the modern harp, because it lacks a front pillar. Instead, the instrument, depicted in paintings more than five thousand years ago, looks like a five- or six-stringed hunting bow. Musicians knelt on the ground and rested the curved part of the bow on their shoulder when playing. Sound boxes, or even drums, were eventually added to the bottom part of the harp to amplify the sound of the strings. Over time, these boxes were enlarged and ornately painted. The bases of Egyptian temple harps were decorated with sphinx heads, and the bow part, which extended up to 6 feet, was decorated with mosaic tiles.

As the harp traveled through other cultures, its shape changed. The angle harp utilizes two posts at a right angle with strings stretched between them. These harps were played in Assyria and ancient Greece.

In the ninth century, the triangular frame harp evolved in medieval Europe and was seen in rock carvings in England and Ireland. These harps differed from earlier instruments in that they were made of three solid parts, in the shape of a triangle, with strings stretched across the middle. The addition of the extra part, known as a forepillar, gave the instrument a more solid construction and greater strength. This, in turn, allowed thicker strings to be used, which gave the harp greater volume and notes that sustained, or rang, for longer periods of time.

The triangular frame harp is believed to have originated in Scandinavia and was brought to northern Europe and the British Isles by Vikings. The word harp comes from an Old Norse word that means "to pluck." This term was widely used for the frame harp by the thirteenth century.

The strings of the harp are enclosed by a frame, and the instrument is supported by a pillar outside the longest string. Harp historian Robert Ruadh describes the ancient instrument, which had thirty to fifty strings and was played by musicians who plucked them with long fingernails:

> The harp played by the Irish and Scottish harpers of the old Gaelic order was an aristocratic instrument, played in the courts of kings and before the chiefs of clans. . . . Its sound-box was carved in one piece out of wood from the bog. It had other-worldly associations, and in the hands of a master harper had power over its listeners to bring them great joy, or cause them to weep with sorrow, or lull them to sleep.[47]

The Concert Harp

The pedal harp used in modern orchestras is a frame harp also known as the concert or grand harp. In the eighteenth century, to broaden the harp's range, pedals were added to raise and lower the strings and produce accidentals—sharp or flat notes outside the seven-note scale.

The average concert grand harp weighs about 90 pounds (40kg) and is slightly more than 6 feet (2m) tall. These are made of maple wood and have forty-six strings, covering six-and-a-half octaves with seven strings per octave. The bass, or lower, strings are made from wound wire, while the treble, or upper, strings are made from gut or nylon. The proper harpist uses only the thumb and first three fingers of each hand to play—the little finger is never used.

Although the harp produces beautiful, "heavenly" music, few composers have written parts for the instrument. It was mainly used for its swirling special effect in operas, although famous composers such as Franz Joseph Haydn, Gioachino Rossini, Frédéric Chopin, and others were accomplished harp players. Wolfgang Amadeus Mozart only used the instrument in one piece, as did Ludwig van Beethoven.

Perhaps the musician who did the most to promote the harp in the twentieth century was, ironically, the outrageous silent comedian Harpo Marx, a member of the renowned Marx Brothers. Marx was a talented, classically

Singer Joanna Newsom performs at the Royal Festival Hall in London, England, in 2010. She uses the harp to create contemporary pop music with a unique and idiosyncratic style.

trained musician who only went into comedy to support his family. His harp performances, however, are memorable moments in classic Marx Brothers movies.

The Merriment of the Lute

In addition to the harp and the lyre, a third type of chordophone, the lute, originated in ancient times. Unlike the harp and the lyre, however, the impact of the lute has been long-lasting. Instruments from the tiny ukulele to the huge stand-up bass owe their basic shape and structure to the ancient lute.

With a neck and fingerboard attached to a shell or drum-like body, the lute had the greatest flexibility of any ancient stringed instrument. Grunfeld describes the importance of the fingerboard:

> [The] principle of the fingerboard, which seems perfectly obvious . . . must have represented a major technological breakthrough in its time. Both the harp and the lyre were designed basically to produce only one note per string . . . to play a variety of tones, one needed a lot of strings. The lute had few strings, but by pressing them against the fingerboard—i.e., by "stopping" the strings—the player had access to a whole gamut of tones. Musically, in an age of melody, the lutes opened up a new range of . . . possibilities.[48]

Like the guitar in later centuries, the ancient lute seems to have been most commonly used to play folk songs, as opposed to martial and religious music. Echoing the excitement attached to rock-and-roll musicians today, expert lute players were considered iconic celebrities. Paintings showed them alongside acrobats, jugglers, snake charmers, and performing monkeys.

By the eighth century, the lute was played throughout the Arab world. The word lute itself is derived from the Arab word *al-'ud*, meaning "wood," so named because it had a soundboard made from wood, as opposed to animal skin, and the body was constructed from wooden strips, rather than a gourd or tortoise shell. An unnamed tenth-century author enthusiastically describes the musician performing an al-'ud recital:

> He played . . . [the strings] in a kind of way that made everyone in the assembly laugh from the merriment and pleasure, joy and gladness, which entered their souls. Then he altered . . . [the strings] and played them in another way, and made them all weep from the sadness of the mode . . . and grief of heart. Then he altered them again, and played them again, and made everyone go to sleep.[49]

The al-'ud was brought to Spain by the Moors during their occupation of that country from 711 to 1492. By the thirteenth century, the instrument had lost its connection to Arab musicians and was widespread throughout Europe. By the sixteenth century, the lute was known as the "Queen of European Instruments."[50]

German and Italian lute makers produced thousands of instruments a year. These generally were made of ash and had long, narrow bodies with nine or eleven broad ribs on the back. The eight to ten strings—arranged in four or five pairs, or courses—were attached at the rounded base by a guitarlike tailpiece. Later a sixth, single string was added. Four to nine frets were attached to the neck so musicians could accurately place their fingers on the fretboard in order to play the proper notes. These frets were made of gut tied around the neck and spaced at chromatic intervals.

Similar to other instruments such as the oboe, lutes were made in many shapes and sizes so that they could be played in different registers. The smallest was the octave lute, followed by the small treble, treble, alto, tenor, bass, and large octave lute.

By the sixteenth century, the popularity of the lute exploded due to the publication of musical instruction books. Danish music historian Hortense Panum explains:

> These lute-books were by no means content with merely giving the public a collection of pieces; in most cases they also gave elaborate instructions for tuning and playing the lute as well as instructions in the art of writing the [music], in fingering, and in the placing of the frets, etc. The text is generally homely and intimate. The reader is always admonished to listen carefully to what is said. The lute-books were also often used to perpetuate moral advice, and even questions of [religious] doctrine.[51]

The lute remained a fashionable instrument for the middle and upper classes throughout the eighteenth century. Johann Sebastian Bach, Haydn, and Mozart added to the already voluminous reams of compositions for the lute. By the end of the eighteenth century, however, the instrument was eclipsed by the violin, guitar, and mandolin. With little fanfare, the instrument that provided the basis for dozens of stringed instruments faded from public view.

The Violin and Viola

The lute was a limited instrument in many ways—it was hard to hear in crowds and, with upwards of two dozen strings in later years, difficult to keep in tune. The four-string violin, on the other hand, was loud, easy to carry, capable of expressing a wide range of musical emotion, and versatile enough to play the most complicated pieces of classical music.

The modern violin has changed little since the Middle Ages. It has the highest pitch of any stringed instrument, except the ukulele, and the four strings are tuned in musical fifths—that is, G, D, A, and E. The strings are attached to four tuning pegs pressed into what is known as a pegbox. Ever since the eighteenth century, the pegbox has been traditionally topped with a carved scroll. An arched back provides the instrument with a great depth of sound, and two f-holes (openings in the shape of the letter F) in the body add to the volume of the violin.

The strings of the violin are played with a bow, a flexible stick about 30 inches (76cm) long, strung with horsehair. While playing the violin, the right-handed musician places the left hand on the fretless neck and presses the strings down on the fingerboard. The right hand and arm are used to draw the bow back and forth at a right angle across the strings.

The Evolution of the Violin

The first bowed instruments were depicted in European illustrations around the tenth century A.D., but the modern violin is a combination of several instruments popular over the next five centuries. It is believed that the first violin was originally adapted from the Moorish rebec, an instrument based on the lute. This pear-shaped instrument was carved and hollowed out from a single block of wood. Around the twelfth century, the medieval fiddle appeared, and this was

A violin made by Antonio Stradivari in Cremona, Italy, in 1699 is on display at the Victoria and Albert Museum in London, England. The modern violin has remained virtually unchanged since the Middle Ages.

constructed from flat pieces of wood formed into a spade shape. Around 1490 the viol appeared in Italy and Spain. This six-string violin-like instrument with frets was played while resting in an upright position on the musician's lap. Italy was also home to the lire da braccio, a seven-stringed instrument that was held under the neck and played with a bow, much like the modern violin.

The names used for the violin show its evolution. The original term comes from *fides*, the Roman word for "strings." This term evolved into *fidicula*, or *vitula* in Medieval Latin, *videle* or *fiedel* in German, *fiddle* in English, and *viola* and *violino* in Italian.

By the time of the Renaissance in the fifteenth century, the violin and viol were the prime instruments of Italy, and the city of Cremona was known as the Town of Violins because so many world-class violin makers worked there. By the 1600s violins were being used more often in orchestras. In 1607 Claudio Monteverdi, a Cremona native who learned to play the viol at age sixteen, transformed music forever by writing the first true opera, *Orfeo*.

By the late seventeenth century, violins and related instruments were favored by composers, orchestras, and conductors. In 1689, one orchestra in Rome reportedly had forty violins, ten violas, seventeen cellos, and seven double basses. (The cello is a large, low-pitched member of the violin family that sounds in the range beneath the violin but above the four-string upright bass, double bass, or contrabass, which is the lowest-pitched member of the violin family.) This orchestra also contained several trumpets, a trombone, and a lute. Conversely, average church trios used only two violins and a bass.

The eighteenth century gave rise to the string quartet, which featured two violins, a cello, and a viola, which was tuned an octave above the cello. Composers such as Bach, Haydn, and Mozart all wrote well-known pieces for quartets.

The eighteenth century also saw advancements in the creation of violins. In the early 1700s, renowned Cremona violin maker Antonio Stradivari made subtle changes in the varnish and structure of his violins to give them a brighter, richer tone. Today, Stradivarius violins are among the most coveted instruments in the world because of their amazing sound quality. In 2011, a Stradivarius made in 1721 sold for nearly $16 million.

The Country Fiddle

By the nineteenth century, the violin was one of the most common instruments in the world, and its popularity drove the viol out of fashion. Orchestras were often half composed of violin players, and the instrument was played by rich and poor alike. In Europe, the Romani people used the instrument for rousing folk music. In the United States, pioneers

The Mandolin

The mandolin, popular in bluegrass and folk music, evolved from the mandora, a small lute with a short neck and eight strings. In the fourteenth century, the mandora was used to play high notes and fill out the sound of lute ensembles. The first mandolin, a smaller version of the mandora called the mandolina, appeared in Italy in the sixteenth century. This instrument had a bowl-shaped body and was brought in great numbers to the United States by southern and eastern European immigrants in the mid-1800s. During this era, families often whiled away the hours playing music on mandolins, guitars, zithers, and ukuleles. By the late 1890s, mail-order companies such as Montgomery Ward and Sears were selling thousands of mandolins every year.

In 1902 instrument maker Orville Gibson did away with the bowl-back mandolin and redesigned the instrument, which made it easier to hold and play. This change resulted in the pear-shaped Gibson A-4 with an arched top and a flat back. Gibson also introduced the Florentine or F-style, which had a decorative scroll near the neck and f-holes carved into the top. Over the decades, other manufacturers imitated Gibson's innovations, but the Gibson F-5, which sold for $4,600 in 2012, was the most popular mandolin for bluegrass musicians. The $3,600 A-5 style was coveted for use in folk, classical, and Irish music.

played violins at Saturday night barn dances to accompany jigs, reels, waltzes, and quadrilles.

By the twentieth century, the versatile violin was widely referred to in the United States as the fiddle, and it played an important role in the record and radio industries. In 1922 the first million-selling country music records were old-time fiddle tunes: "Turkey in the Straw," "The Wreck of Old 97," and "Sallie Gooden." By the end of the 1920s *The Grand Ole Opry,* which featured old time fiddle music, was one of the most popular radio shows in the country.

In 1938 the fiddle was featured in a new style of country music called bluegrass, invented by Bill Monroe. Bluegrass featured old-time fiddle tunes, gospel songs, and country standards that were often performed double time. Fiddlers in Monroe's band, the Bluegrass Boys, were highly skilled at playing rapid-fire cascades of notes that brought audiences to their feet.

Since the early days of *The Grand Ole Opry,* fiddles have been closely associated with country music. Fiddles have also been used to great effect in pop, rock, blues, and even alternative music. As one of the most versatile stringed instruments, the violin has found a place in almost every form of music.

The Standup Bass

While the violin took center stage in the twentieth century, its oversized cousin, the contrabass, was less prominent but just as important. Standing more than 6 feet (2m) tall, the contrabass is the largest member of the violin family, with construction nearly identical to the violin.

The contrabass is referred to by many names including the standup bass, string bass, and bass fiddle. In the 1950s, jazz players jokingly referred to the instrument as the doghouse due to its large wooden body that could presumably act as a home for a canine.

The standup bass can be played with a bow or plucked with the fingers. In the late 1940s, bluegrass and early rock musicians developed a playing style in which they used four fingers to slap the strings, making them click on the instrument's long neck. While the low notes of the instrument may not be as loud as the high-pitched violin, the standup bass lays down the rhythmic foundation behind many styles of

Grammy winner Esperanza Spalding is an accomplished bassist who plays the standup bass as well as the bass guitar.

music. In the 1950s, rock records by singer Elvis Presley featured the driving slap bass of Bill Black. In the 1960s, jazz prodigy Charles Mingus combined gospel, rhythm and blues, and improvised jazz styles into an unequaled bass sound.

The standup bass lost popularity in the 1960s, but the instrument experienced a one-woman twenty-first century revival in the hands of singer, composer, and bassist Esperanza Spalding. In 2010 twenty-six-year-old Spalding won a Grammy for her album *Chamber Music Society*. On the record, Spalding covers tango, samba, jazz, and pop with finger-popping bass breaks and melodic bowing. *Chamber Music Society*, which sold well with both jazz and mainstream audiences, put the standup bass front and center for the first time in decades.

The Early Guitar

Like the standup bass, the bodies of ancient guitars often had hourglass shapes, but it was not until 1265 that the instrument was specifically mentioned in books or poems. By the sixteenth century, the guitar was a staple of Spanish music and commonly found throughout Europe.

The guitar is a plucked chordophone with a neck. It is about 3 feet long and often has a flat back, an hourglass shape, and a flat piece called a headstock at the end of the neck, to which tuning pegs are attached. Modern guitars have six strings. On Spanish, or classical, guitars the strings are made from gut or nylon, with the thickest strings made from silk spun over metal. On other acoustic and electric guitars, the strings are made from steel, nickel-plated steel, and bronze. They are tuned—from lowest to highest—to the notes E, A, D, G, B, and E.

The strings are stretched over a fingerboard that has metal frets. Atop the neck is the tuning head. Classical and acoustic guitars are generally made with a spruce top, or soundboard, and a hardwood back. When the strings are strummed or plucked, the sound emanates from a round hole in the soundboard. Right-handed players use their hand to produce sound with their fingers, fingernails, or

picks while the left hand stops the strings behind the frets to make notes and chords.

The guitar provides musicians with the ability to play loud, ringing chords, single-note lead patterns, or plucked melodies utilizing several strings at a time. Guitar historian Tony Bacon describes the flexibility of the instrument:

> The guitar is a unique musical instrument; no other combines in such a portable package such inherent harmonic, melodic and rhythmic potential. Even played on its own, the guitar offers a remarkable range of harmony to the player, who has continuous access to over three octaves (four on many modern electrics), with [musical sounds] limited only by the guitarist's dexterity and the musical context.[52]

Throughout the centuries, these features have made the instrument extremely popular. For example, an average of 1.5 million guitars is sold every year, compared with around 375,000 woodwinds and 142,000 pianos.

A flamenco dancer performs to music played on a Spanish guitar—also known as classical guitar— an instrument that was in widespread use in Spain and throughout Europe by the sixteenth century.

Pleasant to Hear, Easy to Learn

The guitar evolved from the lute by the 1300s after it was imported to Spain by the Moors. At that time, there were two types of guitars: the almond-shaped guiterre morische, or Moorish guitar, and the hourglass-shaped guitterre latine, or Latin guitar. The guitterre latine had three pairs, or courses, of similarly tuned strings, plus a single high string. These were tuned, from lowest to highest: C, F, A, and D.

By the 1600s the first books of guitar notation, known as tablature, were published for the four-course, or eight-string, guitar in Spain. These instruction books helped boost the popularity of the guitar, which between the sixteenth and nineteenth centuries began to challenge the status of the lute, particularly in Spain, Italy, and France. In 1626 author and guitar player Luis de Briçeño explained why the instrument was so fashionable:

> The guitar is . . . convenient and appropriate to singing, playing, ballet-dancing, jumping, running, folk-dancing and shoedancing. I can serenade with it, singing and expressing with its help a thousand amorous passions. . . . [The guitar] whether well played or badly played, well strung or badly strung, is pleasant to hear and listen to; being so easy to learn, it attracts the busiest of talented people and makes them put aside loftier occupations so that they may hold a guitar in their hands. . . . They desert the lute, mandora, harp, violin, sinfonia, lyre, the orbo, cittern, and clavichord, all for the guitar. Many things could be said in favor of these instruments, but here one consideration is paramount: two thousand people now entertain themselves and express their thoughts and troubles through the guitar.[53]

As more people learned to play the guitar—including French king Louis XIV and English king Charles II—the instrument underwent many changes. A fifth course was added around 1600 and a sixth by the end of the 1700s. Around 1800 these double-string courses were replaced by single strings, and the modern tuning became standard.

During the last half of the nineteenth century, guitar maker Antonio de Torres Jurado produced a lighter guitar with a more resonant sound that resembled today's modern

The Banjo

On the website Bluegrass Banjo, Bill Reese describes the history of the banjo:

Banjos belong to a family of instruments that is very old. Drums with strings stretched over them can be traced throughout the Far East, the Middle East and Africa, almost from the beginning. . . . The banjo, as we can begin to recognize it, was made by African slaves, based on instruments that were indigenous to their parts of Africa. These early "banjos" were spread to the colonies of those countries engaged in the slave trade. Scholars have found that many of these instruments have names that are related to the modern word "banjo," such as "banjar," "banjil," "banza," "bangoe," "bangie," "banshaw." . . . White men began using black-face as a comic gimmick before the American Revolution. The banjo became a prop for these entertainers, either individually or in groups. . . . From the 1840s through the 1890s the minstrel show was not the only place to see banjo players.

There are records of urban banjo contests and tournaments held at hotels, race tracks and bars, especially in New York, to the enthusiastic cheering and clapping of sometimes inebriated crowds. . . . During most of this time, the banjo was looked-down upon by the more well-to-do classes of the population. Articles in the papers of the day, like that in the Boston *Daily Evening Voice* of 1866, classified the banjo of the 1840s and 1850s as an instrument in "the depth of popular degradation," an instrument fit only for "the jig-dancing lower classes of the community. . . . " By 1866, however, the instrument had become a "universal favorite," with over 10,000 instruments in use in Boston alone.

Bill Reese. "Thumbnail History of the Banjo." Bluegrass Banjo, February 15, 1998. http://bluegrassbanjo.org/banhist.html.

instrument. He also got rid of the troublesome tied-on gut frets and replaced them with metal or ivory.

Meanwhile the guitar moved to U.S. shores and was a favorite instrument, along with the banjo, of African American musicians in the rural South. Being poor, many black musicians made their own guitars from boxes and lumber. Blues legend Muddy Waters explained, "All the

Steel Guitar

Steel guitar is a method of playing guitar that takes its name from the steel bar players use to change the pitch of the strings. (Slide bars may also be made of glass or other materials.) The steel guitar style evolved in Hawaii during the nineteenth century when indigenous musicians imitated the sounds of ocean waves and wind by sliding the steel bar up and down the guitar neck with one hand and plucking the strings with the other.

Guitars played with a slide bar and held horizontally with the strings pointed upward are called steel guitars. A steel guitar with eight strings is called a lap steel because it is played while positioned on the lap of the player. In the mid-1930s an electrified version of the steel guitar was built with pickups that could be plugged into a guitar amplifier. This kind of guitar became popular in the southern and western states and was the defining sound of western swing music played by Bob Wills and the Texas Playboys.

Steel guitars used open tunings fixed in one key, prompting players to add a second neck tuned to a different key. This made the guitars heavier, so thin metal legs were added, creating what is called a table steel guitar. In another innovation, foot pedals and knee levers were attached to the table steel, turning it into the pedal steel guitar. These additions allowed the player to raise or lower the pitch of a string by depressing the pedal or moving the knee lever. Pedal steel guitars remain an extremely popular fixture in country music.

kids make they own git-tars [guitars]. Made mine out of a box and a bit of stick for a neck. Couldn't do much with it, but you know, that's how you learn."[54]

The guitar also followed pioneers west across the plains, and was popular with cowboys and rural farmers. Eventually, guitarists playing black blues music mixed it up with white country twang, or "hillbilly" music, and rock and roll was born.

The Electric Guitar

In the twentieth century, sophisticated musicians such as Django Reinhardt and Charlie Christian were able to wring incredible jazz music from the guitar. In the 1930s Christian became one of the first professional musicians to use an electric guitar. With its ability to be amplified louder than brass and percussion instruments, the electric guitar was rapidly incorporated into jazz, western swing, and blues bands. To meet the demand for electric guitars, the Rickenbacker company of Santa Ana, California, began to manufacture electric guitars commercially in 1932. The first Rickenbacker electric was called the "Frying Pan," because the small, round, aluminum body resembled a cooking implement.

Electric guitars rely on an electromagnetic device known as a pickup, which acts as a microphone to transmit the vibration of the strings through a wire cord to an amplifier. The tone and volume of the pickup are controlled on the guitar by knobs that may be adjusted. While the first electric guitars had only one pickup, modern guitars may have up to five, with two or three being standard. Pickups come in a variety of wiring configurations, some geared for lead guitar sounds, others for rhythm or bass tones.

In the late 1960s rock legend Jimi Hendrix used his Fender Stratocaster to push the electric guitar into new musical territory.

After the initial development, companies such as Gibson began making the Electric Spanish guitar in the mid-1930s. This guitar resembled a standard instrument, except that it had f-holes and a pickup attached near the bridge. With the advent of rock and roll in the 1950s, the popularity of the electric guitar skyrocketed. In Fullerton, California, instrument maker Leo Fender redesigned the guitar for the modern age. The Fender Broadcaster was solid wood with a bolt-on neck made for mass production. The guitar was solid ash and had a three-way switch to allow the player to choose combinations between the treble pickup and the bass pickup.

The Broadcaster was soon renamed the Telecaster and remains in production today, along with the wildly popular three-pickup Fender Stratocaster, first produced in 1954. The "Strat" features a vibrato, or "whammy," bar built into the bridge, which allows players to rapidly change the pitch of the strings.

With rock heroes such as Buddy Holly, Elvis Presley, and Chuck Berry all wielding electric guitars on stage, hundreds of thousands of kids picked up guitars in the mid-1950s. Guitar sales in 1950 were about 228,000. By 1959 that number jumped to four hundred thousand. In 1963 alone the number of guitars sold doubled from the year before—from three hundred thousand to six hundred thousand. By 1965 that number had soared to 1.5 million, and Fender alone was selling 1,500 guitars a week.

In the late 1960s Jimi Hendrix was producing music from his Strat that was as unearthly as it was unique. Hendrix milked an infinite range of sounds from his guitar and amp, including screeching feedback, distorted fuzz tone, and other effects. Hendrix proved that the electric guitar could transcend almost any musical boundaries.

The Electric Bass

While Fender cemented his place in history with his six-string electric guitars, he was also the first to mass produce the four-string electric bass guitar. The instrument was meant to duplicate the sound of the standup bass but

The Bass Guitar

When Leo Fender invented the electric bass guitar in 1951, he deliberately designed an uncomplicated instrument. With four strings, one pickup, one volume knob, and one tone knob, the Precision Bass was simple to manufacture and easy to play. Fender celebrated the sixtieth birthday of the Precision in 2011, and the instrument remains popular with bass players throughout the world.

After Fender introduced its electric bass guitar, other companies such as Rickenbacker and Gibson brought their own basses to the market. These companies made some minor changes to the bass, such as moving the pickup closer to the neck and creating different body styles. Real innovations did not occur in the bass guitar until the early 1970s when Alembic, Inc., began designing expensive custom instruments, or boutique basses, for Phil Lesh of the Grateful Dead. Alembic added built-in electronics that gave the instrument greater volume and tonal variation.

In 1975 Alembic added a fifth string to the bass, a low B to supply extra deep notes. By the 1980s the popularity of five-string basses was firmly established, and by the 1990s a sixth string, a high C, was added to some bass guitars. In the 2000s synthetic materials, digital circuitry, and acoustic/electric basses were available as Leo Fender's simple idea continued to change with the times.

looked and played like an electric guitar. The first Fender bass, called the Precision Bass, was produced in 1951. With its electric guitar pickup, the instrument could thunder when plugged into an amplifier. This allowed bass players to take a more dominant role in bands, and the Precision quickly became a standard element of jazz, rock, blues, and country music.

In 1960 Fender introduced a second model, the Jazz Bass, which had a brighter tone than the Precision due to the configuration of its pickups. By the end of the 1960s bass players such as Jack Bruce of Cream and Noel Redding of the Jimi Hendrix Experience were using their Fender bass guitars to play intricate riffs and complex runs that rivaled those played by lead guitar players.

From the relaxing sounds of a quietly plucked lute in ancient Greece to the rumbling crescendo of the bass guitar, stringed instruments have changed the sounds of music for thousands of years. Whether played in love songs of the Italian Renaissance or modern-day rock music, the sounds made by lutes, violins, cellos, banjos, mandolins, guitars, and other chordophones have guided listeners through emotional highs and lows for centuries.

CHAPTER 5

Keyboards

Wind, percussion, and stringed instruments have been popular throughout the centuries because they are relatively simple to make and easy to carry. On the other hand, keyboards such as organs, harpsichords, and pianos are late arrivals to the family of instruments, because they are complicated to play, expensive to make, and sometimes nearly impossible to move. The modern piano, for example, weighs an average of about 500 pounds (226kg) and has nearly 10,000 separate parts, compared with 150 parts in a valve trumpet and less than half that many in an acoustic guitar.

Keyboards are defined as musical instruments in which sound is produced by a vibrator that is activated mechanically or electronically by a person striking keys, levers, or foot pedals. The vibrator may be strings in a piano and harpsichord, or pipes in an organ. The movement of the players fingers, hands, and feet supply the mechanical force to strike or pluck the strings, or activate air to vibrate pipes in an organ.

The Ancient Organ

Like many other modern instruments, the first keyboards were made from a combination of several primitive instruments joined together. For example, the early organ

consisted of a wind instrument—the trumpet—joined with a forced-air concept seen on bagpipes. Those two inventions were joined on the ancient organ, known as the hydraulos (literally "water flute"), invented in Alexandria, Egypt, around 246 B.C. by an inventor named Ctesibius. The instrument consisted of a wind pump—a vase with a close-fitting movable valve inside that could be filled with water. The valve forced air through a hole in the bottom of the vase into several differently pitched flutes or trumpets. Metal sliders under each horn were pushed in by the finger, thus allowing air into specific pipes. Each produced a loud musical note. The mechanical sliders had springs that closed them when not in use. Later the sliders were attached to a keyboard mechanism—that is, a set of levers or keys laid out in a row that could be struck by the fingers.

Several centuries after Ctesibius invented the hydraulos, the Romans replaced the vase mechanism with human power. Male slaves were ordered to blow into a large wooden box known as an air-storage chest. The stored air could be let out under controlled conditions to play pipes fitted with reeds. Later, the blowpipes were replaced by pleated leather bags called bellows, which could be pumped up and down to produce strong blasts of air. This instrument was called an organon, a term that the Greeks used to describe tools used for work. Keyboard historian C.F. Abdy Williams describes the role of the organon in ancient Roman society:

> The instrument which began in this humble manner not only became exceedingly popular, but was for centuries a source of admiration and astonishment to the unlearned. The powerful sound, the rapidity of execution, the mysterious bubbling of the water, the exertions of the slaves, who were obliged to pump with all their might to supply the air in sufficient quantity, all combined to attract attention to it. It was used for contests in the public games; it formed part of the entertainment at feasts; it found its way into private houses; and in one instance, at least, took the place of the trumpet in giving the signal for the commencement of the brutal . . . sea-fights, which were the delight of the . . . populace.[55]

By the tenth century A.D., organs were found in churches throughout Europe. The Benedictine monk Theophilus describes a German instrument in the 1100s that had eight copper pipes, an air-storage (or wind) chest, a wind collector, and lettered wooden sliders for each pipe that allowed the player to know which notes he was hitting.

Pedals, Pipes, and Stops

By the Middle Ages, the organ had grown into one of the most complex machines ever invented until that time. Wind chests were able to house dozens of pipes, and because a method was needed to play the multiple pipes, extra keyboards were added, with some organs featuring two or three keyboards along with a set of foot pedals to play bass notes. The development of sliders that moved under more than one pipe meant that one key could play multiple pipes, giving the organ the ability to play a single note with several different pipes for various octaves.

By 1450, some German church organs had from six to twenty-six pipes per note. Mechanisms called stops (push-pull knobs set near the keyboard) allowed players to shut off

The Sound "Heard Everywhere"

In the tenth century, a monk named Wulfstan described the labor of workers called organ-blowers. These men pumped the twenty-eight large bellows attached to the great pipe organ in Winchester Cathedral in England:

> Seventy strong men operate [the bellows], flexing their arms, dripping with sweat; and they eagerly exhort their companions to drive the air upward with all their force so that the swelling reservoir may resound with full chamber. It in turn sustains the four hundred pipes by itself, which the hand guided by musical skill controls: it is the hand which opens closed pipes and again closes open ones, as the melody of the music requires. . . . Like thunder the iron-clad sound strikes one's ears so that they can take in no sound save this: the sound, reverberating here and there, is so loud that everyone covers his open ears with his hands; as he draws near he can in no way endure the roar in which the various pipes produce as they sound. The music of the pipes is heard everywhere through the town, and its flying report traverses the entire country.

Quoted in Michael Lapidge and John Crook, et al. *The Cult of St Swithun, Volume 4, Part 2.* Oxford, England: Oxford University Press, 2003, pp. 384–384.

specific pipes or add them to the chorus of notes. Unique tone colors and sound effects were made by the addition of reeds, square wooden pipes, and other inventions that were controlled by the stops. Organ scholar Bernard Sonnaillon describes the sounds produced by the instrument:

[Some pipes] seek to imitate various sounds such as birdcalls, animal cries and the sounds of nature and of warfare: the Rossignol or Nachtigall [stops], whose tiny pipes are suspended in water so that bubbles produced by the flow of air imitate the warbling of nightingales; a barking dog, a growling bear or a braying ass produced by untuned pipes; a storm created by a mechanism (a length of wood) which holds down the lowest notes of the pedals simultaneously; the sound of beating rain suggested by means of small pebbles rolling around inside a metal drum; military percussion (Banda militare) incorporating the big drum and cymbals, or the rolling of kettledrums (Timpani) produced by means of two untuned pipes, and, finally, the Chapeau chinois in which small spherical bells are shaken against a rod, and the Zimbelstern which consists of a revolving metal star with a set of bells attached to it.[56]

Despite these later additions, the organ of 1450 differed little from the pipe organs in use today, as organ authority Nicholas Thistlewaite explains: "It is a remarkable tribute to the medieval enterprise and craftsmanship that no

Organ technicians work on the 9,999-pipe organ at Royal Albert Hall in London, England, in 1962. The process of re-tuning the organ requires that each piece be taken apart and cleaned individually and can take seven to ten years to complete.

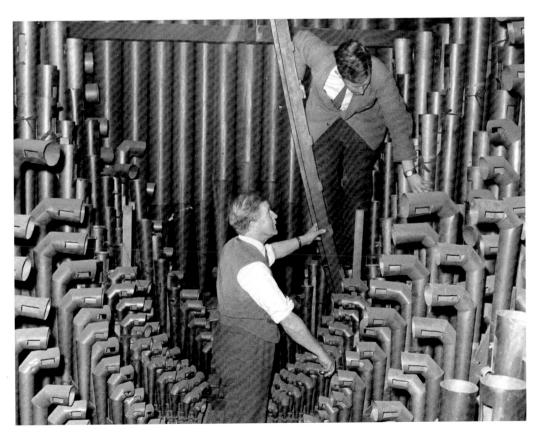

significant innovations in the basic design of the organ were made for the next three centuries."[57]

As the organ grew in complexity, it also expanded in size. By the second half of the eighteenth century, several European churches contained spectacular organs that drew worshipers from near and far. Organ builders—some of the most respected craftsmen of their time—traveled from town to town constructing huge, expensive organs as churches competed to outdo one another.

Bach's "Feet Had Wings"

During the early years of the eighteenth century, Johann Sebastian Bach was one of Germany's most renowned organists. In addition to writing music for the instrument, Bach built and repaired organs, and his mastery of the instrument is legendary. After watching him test a restored organ in Cassel, Germany, rector Constantin Bellermann commented on Bach's incredible footwork:

> [Bach] can by the use of his feet alone (while his fingers do either nothing or something else) achieve such an admirable, agitated, and rapid concord of sounds on the church organ that others would seem unable to imitate it even with their fingers. When he was called . . . to Cassel to pronounce an organ properly restored, he ran over the pedals with this same facility, as if his feet had wings, making the organ resound with such fullness, and so penetrate the ears of those present like a thunderbolt, that . . . [the] Prince of Cassel admired him with such astonishment that he drew a ring with a precious stone from his finger and gave it to Bach as soon as the sound had died away. If Bach earned such a gift for the agility of his feet, what, I ask, would the Prince have given him if he had called his hands into service as well.[58]

Bach also wrote more than 260 organ compositions in his lifetime. Although he never traveled more than 100 miles (161km) from his home in central Germany, the composer synthesized the German organ styles with those from France and Italy, changing organ music forever.

Partially in response to the complexity of Bach's music,

as well as that of other composers, the organ continued to undergo changes in tone and structure. In the nineteenth century, pipes that imitated orchestral instruments were developed. These instruments inspired composers such as Franz Liszt and Max Reger to write new orchestral music for the organ.

In 1935 an entirely different sort of organ was invented in the United States by Laurens Hammond, who utilized electronic circuits, vacuum tubes, and amplifiers to produce tones similar to a pipe organ. Although not really a true organ because it does not vibrate air within a pipe, the Hammond became popular with traveling musicians, dance bands, and amateur musicians who could, for the first time, buy compact organs to play at home. By the 1960s and 1970s, the electric organ was a fixture in rhythm and blues, rock and roll, and soul bands. For example, the British group Procol Harum used the Hammond to great effect on the 1967 hit "A Whiter Shade of Pale."

The Clavichord

Before the Hammond organ was invented, only large churches and mansions of the rich and powerful could accommodate the pipes, pedals, sound chests, and numerous keyboards found on the pipe organ. Average families could not afford their own keyboard instruments until the 1500s, when instrument innovators produced the clavichord. The instrument was made by joining the parts of two instruments: the keys from the organ and the strings and frame from the ancient harp-like psaltery.

The clavichord's Latin name explains its function—*clavis*, or key, and *chorde*, or string. The early clavichord was light and portable, not much bigger than a piece of luggage. It had a rectangular case with a keyboard on the left and a soundboard with twenty strings on the right. Thin metal strings running parallel to the ground are attached on the right to tuning pins that can be turned to raise or lower the pitch. The strings run over a bridge set in the soundboard and are fixed solidly to the instrument by devices known as hitchpins set on the left side of the case. Early clavichords

Zithers and Dulcimers

Before the Hammond was invented, only churches and the castles of the rich and powerful could accommodate the pipes, sound chests, and numerous keyboards found on the pipe organ. Beginning around the seventeenth century, however, musicians could obtain smaller keyboard instruments that could easily fit into the corner of a room. Similar to the organ, the harpsichord—forerunner to the piano—was based on an ancient instrument, in this case the zither.

The most primitive zithers were made from gut strings attached to bars and stretched over holes in the ground—the hole being necessary to resonate the sound of the strings. The ground zither evolved into board zithers and more complex instruments made from bone, stone, or reed tubes. Hollow gourds were attached to act as resonators. Like later zithers, these instruments had strings stretched between two bridges, and the strings were plucked or struck with sticks or other hammers.

By 1100 B.C., long, slim, fretted zithers with silk strings were played in China. A similar instrument, the 6-foot-long koto, is still played in Japan. A ten-string, zitherlike instrument was known as the psaltery in Turkey in the 1100s (A.D.), and by the fourteenth century, the instrument had grown to encompass sixty-six strings arranged in groups of three. The dulcimer (in Latin *dulce melos*, or "sweet song") was similar to the psaltery but had strings that were meant to be played with two small padded hammers, much as piano hammers strike strings. By the seventeenth century, dulcimers were very popular among troubadours and minstrels.

One of the most talented players was Pantaleon Hebenstreit of Eisleben, Germany. As piano scholar David Crombie writes:

> [Hebenstreit] became a famous dulcimer player, wielding the instrument's hammers with a degree of showmanship that made [him] a celebrity across Europe. . . . A good dulcimer player would . . . have had considerable control over both the volume and tone of each individual note played, and could introduce their own expression into any piece of music. That is exactly what made Hebenstreit famous. Such was Hebenstreit's fame as a dulcimer virtuoso that he set about redesigning the instrument to suit his talents. He greatly enlarged the instrument so that it was more than nine feet [2.74m] long, four times the usual size. He increased its range by providing 180 strings, and added an extra soundboard. In order to give himself a yet wider tonal spectrum he developed double-faced hammers, where each face was covered with different materi-

als so that he could choose between a hard and a soft impact upon the strings. . . . The instrument incorporated a dynamic range unusual at the time, but the skills required to play it meant that few could master it, and its complexity and size meant that still fewer were attracted to own one. . . . But its influence was considerable . . . and is an important link between the world of keyed and non-keyed stringed instruments.

David Crombie. *Piano*. San Francisco: GPI, 1995, p. 7.

An 1885 photograph depicts a young Japanese woman playing a traditional koto, or Japanese harp. The koto is an example of a zither—an instrument with strings stretched on a flat body.

had twenty notes, with more added in the fifteenth century. By the sixteenth century, the instrument encompassed two and a half octaves, and by the seventeenth that number had grown to four octaves.

When the clavichord key was depressed, a small brass blade called a tangent rises up and strikes a string, making it vibrate and produce sound. When the key is released, the string is immediately silenced by a piece of felt woven through the strings near the hitchpins. Players can produce vibrato, or fluctuations in pitch, by varying the pressure on the keys.

The felt, combined with the instrument's small soundboard, gives the clavichord a very quiet sound, which made it popular in monasteries and nunneries, where the soft music would not disturb others. Because of its small size and low cost, the instrument was also used for teaching and was fashionable at intimate gatherings in the homes of average citizens. While the clavichord is associated with Renaissance music, an amplified version of the instrument, the clavinet, was popularized by soul singer Stevie Wonder in the 1970s. After Wonder used the clavinet on hit singles such as "Superstition" and "Higher Ground," the instrument became a fixture in 1970s funk and disco music.

The harpsichord used by Austrian composer Wolfgang Amadeus Mozart is on display in Prague, Czech Republic. It stands in the same room where Mozart used to stay and compose at the Bertramka Villa.

Harpsichords

Unlike the clavichord, the harpsichord produced a louder tone because its strings were plucked by a *plectrum*, or pick, made from a quill or cowhide. Musicians and composers who desired instruments for concert and ensemble use preferred the harpsichord, which was widely used from the 1700s to the early 1800s.

The clear, crisp, and clean sounds of the harpsichord's plucked metal strings made it perfect for the complex sounds of contrapuntal music—that

Quills and the Harpsichord

The strings of the harpsichord are plucked by quills made from feathers. Music professors Murray Campbell, Clive Greated, and Arnold Myers explain how quills are made and used on the instrument:

On a harpsichord, the quill is a crucial component in determining the tone quality, and thus requires special attention from the maker. Raven or vulture feathers are considered best for quill making, but crow feathers are acceptable and more readily available. The largest six or eight feathers from an adult crow are the ones that are used, a single feather being sufficient for three or four plectra [picks]. The feather is cut on a wooden block with a sharp knife at about ten degrees to the surface, to form a similar shape to a pen nib. . . . Once all of the quills have been fixed into the jacks [which are attached to the keys], the complete set is voiced by shaving away small amounts of materials from the undersides. . . . Although most players would claim that the traditional crow or raven's feather quill gives the best sound, this material has some practical disadvantages. Feather plectra wear quite quickly and need continual replacement, and they are also sensitive to changes in humidity.

Murray Campbell, Clive Greated, and Arnold Myers. *Musical Instruments.* Oxford, England: Oxford University Press, 2006, p. 338.

is, music written by composers such as Bach in which two or more melodies were played simultaneously. The volume of the harpsichord came from its long, narrow wing shape that supported a large soundboard and long, thick strings. Each string in a harpsichord has a small plectrum set in a small piece of wood called a jack, which is attached to a key. When the key is depressed, the far end raises the jack and the plectrum plucks the string. When the finger is removed from the key, the plectrum slides down without hitting the string again. With this system, the sound and tone of the instrument remains constant regardless of how much pressure is applied to the key by the musician.

By the sixteenth century two strings were added to each key, one in standard pitch, the other an octave higher. By the 1700s, some harpsichord manufacturers were making large models with up to five strings per note and a second, or even third, keyboard. This allowed players to strike notes in a normal range with one keyboard and strike strings an octave higher or lower with another.

The Early Piano

By the end of the 1600s the keyboard had come a long way from the hydraulos. European citizens were familiar with huge pipe organs, clavichords, harpsichords, and other similar instruments. All of these, however, presented problems for the musician and composer, as piano scholar David Crombie writes:

> Musicians and composers during the eighteenth and nineteenth centuries preferred the harpsichord for concert and ensemble use because of the instrument's loud, clear sounds. None of these gave the player a satisfactory way of controlling dynamics. In other words, it was impossible to control individually the volume of each note played. This made it difficult to introduce expression to the music. There were various ineffective solutions. The organist could change stops to give the instrument a more powerful sound. The harpsichord player could introduce extra sets of strings to make the instrument louder. The clavichord player was able to take some advantage of the instrument's limited degree of dynamic response, but it was such a quiet instrument anyway that playing more softly wasn't of practical use. The only effective way that composers could draw expression from these instruments was by actually writing in more notes when emphasis was required.[59]

The man credited with solving all of these problems on various instruments was harpsichord maker Bartolomeo

Cristofori, father of the pianoforte. Cristofori worked for Prince Ferdinand dé Medici in Florence, Italy. Although there are no records of his first piano, the world's oldest surviving piano, housed in the Metropolitan Museum of Art in New York City, was built by Cristofori in 1720. Historians believe that he constructed the first piano around 1710. Because Cristofori's piano had the ability to resonate with so much more dynamic range than other stringed keyboards at the time, his invention was known as the pianoforte—piano meaning "soft" in Italian, and forte "loud." As Crombie writes, "The combination of the two words emphasizes the piano's potential to produce loud or soft tones depending on how hard its keys are struck."[60]

Cristofori's piano had a four-octave range with courses of strings tuned together. Like modern pianos, when the keys were depressed they activated hammers, which hit the strings. The instrument had some problems, however. For example, sometimes an individual hammer bounced back and hit a string several times when the key was hit only once. Also, the pounding of the hammer tended to break the strings until thicker strings were developed later in the century.

While the pianoforte was clearly groundbreaking, few musicians were skillful enough to play it. Organ and harpsichord players had a difficult time regulating how hard they depressed the keys, and no pianofortes existed outside Florence, Italy. Cristofori built only about twenty pianofortes before he died at the age of seventy-five in 1731.

The English Viennese Schools

By 1760 pianofortes were not made in Italy, but instead were manufactured mainly in Germany, Austria, and England. Some of the best pianos were built by German craftsmen working for the Broadwood Company in London, England. Small models, known as the English Square, cost less than half the price of a standard harpsichord. In the nineteenth century, an unnamed member of the Broadwood family described the characteristics of the English Square:

They were in length about four feet, the hammers very lightly covered with a thin coat of leather; the strings were small, nearly the size of those used on the Harpsichord; the tones clear, what is now called thin and wiry—[the] object being, seemingly, to approach the tones of the Harpsichord, to which the ear, at that period, was accustomed.[61]

By the late 1700s the piano was being made in unique and inventive shapes and sizes. Lightweight boxes with keys, soundboard, strings—and sometimes no legs—were called portable pianos and played by students and traveling musicians. An instrument known as the "sewing box" was a real piano with two and a half octaves. With its 9½-by-13½-inch case about 6 inches tall, it could be set on any table. An instrument known as an orphica had a keyboard and hammers attached to a small harp-like instrument, which could be worn around the neck with a leather strap.

While novelty pianos were popular with the public, the highest-quality instruments were the Viennese pianos, resembling baby grands, built by Johann Andreas Stein. In 1830 composer Friedrich Kalkbrenner described the difference between the pianos made in the Viennese style and those made in London:

> The instruments of Vienna and London have produced two different schools. The pianists of Vienna are especially distinguished for the precision, clearness and rapidity of their execution; the instruments fabricated in that city are extremely easy to play, and, in order to avoid confusion of sound, they are made with mufflers [dampers] up to the last high note; from this results a great dryness in [sustained] passages, as one sound does not flow into another. In Germany the use of the pedals is scarcely known. English pianos possess rounder sounds and a somewhat heavier touch; they have caused the professors of that country to adopt a grander style, and that beautiful manner of singing which distinguishes them; to succeed in this, the use of the loud pedal is indispensable, in order to conceal the dryness inherent to the pianoforte.[62]

Perhaps the most eminent player of the Viennese school was Wolfgang Amadeus Mozart, who learned to play the harpsichord when he was three years old and probably en-

countered his first piano at the age of eighteen. While the composer wrote most of his early sonatas and concertos for the harpsichord, others may have been written with the piano in mind. Whatever the case, the renowned composer was a talented pianist who played in a unique contrapuntal style. Music professor David Rowland explains, "One of the most noteworthy aspects of Mozart's expressive performance was his use of rubato . . . a technique whereby the two hands do not quite synchronize."[63]

With composers such as Mozart leading the way, the piano continued to grow in popularity, especially among nobility and royalty. In the 1790s the grand piano had six octaves—one more than the standard of the day. By the mid-nineteenth century, composers such as Franz Liszt were transforming the way the piano was played, as Crombie writes:

> Liszt was a revolutionary in romantic music and was recognised as the greatest pianist of his day. His playing style both excited and delighted audiences. He became totally engrossed in his playing, and as a result his emotions took control. Coupled with his remarkably strong hands, this resulted in the destruction of many a piano, especially at the beginning of his career when instruments were less robust.[64]

Pianos for the People

Throughout the nineteenth century, instrument makers continued to improve and change the piano. Octaves were added until the piano had eighty-eight keys, and heavier hammers, thicker strings, and iron frames were made to improve durability, loudness, and tone. Away from the concert hall, the piano was seen as an instrument of refinement that even average workers could strive to own. To fill this lucrative market, piano makers began to build smaller, less expensive models for the home. By the end of the century, player pianos came into vogue. These instruments could play automatically, utilizing a long roll of paper with holes punched in it that turned levers to activate hammers on the strings. At first these were cranked by hand, later by electric motors. Taverns and amusement parks featured player pianos that operated only after patrons inserted coins into a pay box.

As pianos became more available to the average citizen, music changed along with the instruments. In the late years of the 1800s, a style called ragtime was developed by African American performers in saloons and minstrel theaters. Written specifically for the piano, ragtime is syncopated music in which the melody is played with the right hand while a "walking" bass line is played with the left. This music was extremely difficult to play—so difficult, in fact, that most of it was disseminated to the general public via player pianos that could be programmed to play the complex tunes. The leading proponent of ragtime was Scott Joplin, whose 1899 composition "Maple Leaf Rag" began the national ragtime craze and went on to sell more than one million copies of sheet music.

After the ragtime fad passed in 1910, other African American jazz musicians continued to revolutionize piano music, including Jelly Roll Morton, who took 1920s jazz to new heights. He achieved great fame with his ability to improvise, or make up melodies on the spot. Morton wrote down his improvisations on sheet music, which helped spread the sound of jazz across the globe. By the late 1940s the pianist Thelonious Monk was creating jazz unlike anything else ever written. Monk specialized in accenting melodies in odd places and ending musical phrases with unexpected notes.

In later years, jazz and blues pianists inspired rock-and-roll players such as "Little Richard" Penniman, Jerry Lee Lewis, and others. Little Richard and Lewis were keyboard prodigies who often used the piano as a prop to get crowds on their feet. While screaming out hits such as "Long Tall Sally," "Good Golly Miss Molly," and "Tutti Frutti," Little Richard was known to pull off his glittering shoes to tickle the keys with his feet. Lewis could get even more outrageous when playing his hit songs "Whole Lotta Shakin' Goin' On" and "Great Balls of Fire." Lewis beat the keys with his boot and pounded out bass notes with his forehead. Nicknamed "The Killer," Lewis also destroyed grand pianos on occasion. He danced on top of the instrument, tore off the keys and tossed them into the audience, and even pushed the heavy instruments off the stage. One time, during "Great Balls of Fire," Lewis poured gasoline over his piano and set it on fire.

While the piano has a shorter history than almost any other musical instrument, it shaped and influenced the sound of music practically from its first incarnation in Cristofori's studio. From the startling opening chords of Ludwig van Beethoven's Ninth Symphony to the rollicking rock of "Tutti Frutti," the hammering notes emitted by the piano's eighty-eight keys continue to inspire and delight more than four centuries after the instrument was born.

CHAPTER 6

Digital Instruments

Throughout the early decades of the twentieth century, musicians adopted the new electrical components made possible by an ongoing technological revolution. The first keyboards with an electric boost were found on the Hammond organ in the 1930s. The instrument generated sound with electric motors called tonewheels, which replaced traditional organ reeds and pipes. The tonewheels rotated in front of pickups similar to those used in electric guitars, and the organ-like sounds were amplified through speakers. In the late 1940s the concept of electronic keyboards was extended to the piano. The sounds of the electronic piano were created by keyboard-operated hammers striking steel reeds similar to xylophone keys. These sounds were amplified by pickups.

Early electric organs and pianos made sounds with moving mechanical parts, making them electro-mechanical devices. While the tones were pleasing, the mechanical parts made the instruments heavy. For example, the Hammond B-3 model organ, which is popular with rock bands even today, weighs around 425 pounds (193kg). The well-loved electric piano, the Fender Rhodes, weighs between 100 and 200 pounds (45 to 90kg) depending on the year it was manufactured. These instruments, with hundreds of moving parts, were also prone to breaking down.

Even as the popularity of electric pianos and organs was growing in the 1950s, some inventors dreamed of generating musical sounds completely by electronic means. There would be no spinning tonewheels, vibrating reeds, or pickups. Instead, the instruments would utilize microprocessors, programmable integrated circuits that evolved over the decades into the microchips found inside all digital devices including synthesizers, drum machines, and computers.

The Voice of Victor

Long before tiny advanced microprocessors could fit inside a keyboard, two pioneering engineers working at RCA Laboratories in Princeton, New Jersey, made the first music with a computer. In 1955 Harry Olson and Herbert Belar created the RCA Mark II Sound Synthesizer, nicknamed Victor. Like other computers of this era, Victor filled a large room with consoles, wires, tubes, knobs, switches, gauges, paper rolls, and blinking lights. Victor created a wide array of musical sounds generated by a device called a vacuum tube oscillator, which modified electrical signals and converted them to various musical frequencies.

In 1955, RCA released the four-record set *The Sounds and Music of the RCA Electronic Music Synthesizer*. Three of the records are filled with dry narration that explains how the machine works. The fourth record contains songs created on Victor, including Johann Sebastian Bach's Fugue No. 2, "Home Sweet Home," and "Blue Skies." While the music sounds more like an old-fashioned calliope pipe organ attached to a merry-go-round, it was the first record of synthesizer music ever released. The narrator concludes accurately, "In the future, synthesis can bring us a totally new experience."[65]

When the Victor sound synthesizer was installed at the Columbia-Princeton Electronic Music Center (now called the Columbia University Computer Music Center) in New York City in 1957, it attracted attention from a number of composers. One of them, Milton Babbitt, released two albums of original compositions, *Vision and Prayer* and *Philomel*, recorded on Victor in the early 1960s. Babbitt was attracted to the synthesizer, because it produced fast-paced music in a mechanical fashion, with a rhythmic and tonal precision not possible on a regular piano.

Moog's Synthesizer

Electrical engineer and physicist Robert Moog also took a keen interest in the Victor synthesizer. Moog, who attended Columbia and studied at the Electronic Music Center, appreciated the Victor, because he was interested in electronic music systems. However, the massive size of the Victor meant it could not be used on stage. Moog wanted to bring electronic music to the public and worked to develop a portable, stage-ready synthesizer that could be mass produced.

Moog was able to realize his vision by drawing upon a relatively new technological breakthrough, the integrated circuit (IC) board, which was first developed in 1958. Integrated

Inventor Robert Moog poses with his pioneering Moog synthesizer, which saw immediate success in popular music after its release in 1967.

Electronic Sound Generation

The temporary effects associated with the rise and fall of a sound are attack, decay, sustain, and release, called the ADSR envelope. Music professors Murray Campbell, Clive Greated, and Arnold Myers explain:

> [When] a note is struck on the piano it takes a certain time for the sound level to build up to its maximum value; once this has been reached it dies quite rapidly even though the key remains depressed. On releasing the key the sound fades away very rapidly, but not instantaneously. These rise and fall times . . . are set on a synthesizer using a unit referred to as an "envelope generator" . . . [which] has four primary controls: "attack," "decay," "sustain," and "release." . . . When the key is pressed the ADSR generator is triggered; its output rises more or less rapidly, depending on the setting of the attack time. When the maximum has been reached the signal level falls back to a constant voltage, determined by the setting of the sustain level. The time for the signal to fall back to the sustain level is known as the decay time and is set by a separate control. On key release the signal dies completely in a time determined by the setting of the release time.

Murray Campbell, Clive Greated, and Arnold Myers. *Musical Instruments.* Oxford, England: Oxford University Press, 2006, pp. 445–446.

circuits, or chips, are made with a series of transistors, electronic devices that switch the flow of electricity off and on, or amplifying current. Moog used the ICs as electronic oscillators. An oscillator creates raw sounds with a timbre shaped by electronic signals called sound waves. The signals are called sine waves, square waves, sawtooth waves, and triangle waves. Some are defined by the shape of the sound wave they produce. For example, a sawtooth wave resembles the blade of a rip saw; the sound ramps up slowly and drops sharply. A square wave alternates instantly between two sound levels, a high and a low state.

Moog's synthesizer combined various waveforms to produce complex sounds that could mimic sounds of existing instruments such as the acoustic guitar. When a person plays an acoustic instrument, the sound is broken up into four phases, which occur in very rapid succession: attack, decay, sustain, and release, called the ADSR envelope. Attack is the time it takes for a note to go from silence to peak volume, decay is the rundown from the peak, sustain is the length of the note's duration, and release is the time the note takes to go from sustain level to silence. Moog's synthesizer used electronic means to control the ADSR envelope, while using circuits to alter frequency, volume, and other aspects of the sound. The Moog synthesizer also utilized a large number of dials and switches to control specific circuits, and therefore the overall sound of the instrument.

Because the musician had direct control of each circuit, the early Moog was an analog synthesizer. Music professor Geoffrey Stanton explains the sound of analog synthesizers: "The key advantages of early analog systems included warm, vibrant sound quality with great versatility and flexibility in control."[66]

Strange Days

While the technology behind the synthesizer was complex, the invention came along at a perfect time. The first commercial models of the Moog synthesizer appeared in 1967, during the middle of the hippie counterculture revolution. Popular bands such as the Doors, the Beatles, and the Rolling Stones were pushing musical boundaries and embellishing their music with a wide array of instruments not previously used in rock, including the Indian sitar, the concert harp, and the lute-like tambura.

Bands were attracted to the Moog synthesizer because it could be used to create short, memorable licks that grabbed the listener's attention. It could also be used to enhance or distort vocals as the Doors demonstrated on "Strange Days," the first major rock song to feature the Moog. "Strange Days," with its swirling, carnival-like organ and dark lyrics about alienation, hit number one in October 1967. The unsettling effect of the song was heighted by lead vocalist Jim Morrison's singing, which was processed through a Moog. This gave the voice a foreboding feel as Doors' drummer John Densmore wrote, "We certainly made Jim's voice sound 'strange' on 'Strange Days.'"[67]

In the months that followed the release of "Strange Days," the Moog was featured on the Rolling Stones' album *Their Satanic Majesties Request,* Simon and Garfunkel's *Bookends,* and the Byrds' *The Notorious Byrd Brothers.* Perhaps the most groundbreaking Moog-based record was the 1968 album *Switched-On Bach* by Wendy Carlos, who used the synthesizer to play classical masterpieces such as Bach's Brandenburg Concerto and *The Well-Tempered Clavier.* While the Moog sounds primitive, it was very effective, as music reviewer Bruce Eder explains:

> Carlos' use of the Moog's oscillations, squeaks, drones, chirps, and other sounds was highly musical in ways that ordinary listeners could appreciate . . . and was characterized by—for the time—amazing sensitivity and finely wrought nuances, in timbre, tone, and expressiveness. Carlos saw the Moog voice as valid on its own terms, which may be one reason why this album still stands out today . . . and the Moog is working in its own "voice," rather than overtly imitating other, non-electronic instruments.[68]

After the commercial breakthrough of *Switched-On Bach,* the Moog synthesizer continued to make inroads in popular music. In 1970 the instrument was featured on several songs from the Beatles' final album *Abbey Road,* including "Because," "Here Comes the Sun," and "I Want You (She's So Heavy)." The progressive rock trio Emerson, Lake and Palmer also featured the Moog prominently on its biggest hit "Lucky Man." Keyboardist Keith Emerson toured with five Moog synthesizers, including a smaller version of the instrument, the forty-four-key Minimoog, which resembled a small portable organ. In 1971 Carlos once again used the Moog to transform classical music. Hired by director Stanley Kubrick to create a soundtrack for the ultra-violent science fiction movie *A Clockwork Orange*, Carlos created futuristic versions of Ludwig van Beethoven's "Ode to Joy," Gioachino Rossini's "William Tell Overture," and other well-known classics.

The Roland Synthesizer

Moog manufactured a limited number of expensive analog synthesizers that were largely sold to professional musicians. The instrument was not widely available to the public until 1973 when the Japanese Roland Corporation released the first inexpensive mass-produced analog synthesizer: the SH-1000. The Roland SH-1000 was slightly smaller than the Minimoog. Rather than design the instrument for the stage, Roland made the easy-to-operate synthesizer for amateurs. Unlike all Moog models, which required musicians to program individual sounds, the Roland had ten preset sounds that could be turned on and off by pressing color-coded selector tabs. The instrument also had various knobs and volume sliders for more advanced sound creation.

Roland soon released the SH-2000, a more advanced model with thirty preset sounds including the tuba, trombone, flute, clarinet, saxophone, violin, cello, bass guitar, fuzz guitar, piano, and harpsichord. The instrument also made unusual sounds with names such as Popcorn, Space Reed, Planet, Frog Man, Funny Cat, Growl, Wow, and Wind. This more advanced synthesizer appealed to professionals, and by the mid-1970s Roland synthesizers could be heard on hit records by Human League, Blondie, The Band, Roxy Music, and Jethro Tull.

Early Rolands, along with the Moogs, were monophonic, meaning they could only play one note at a time. In 1975 Moog introduced the Polymoog, a seventy-one-key polyphonic synthesizer that allowed musicians to play more than a single note or melody at one time. While organs, pianos, guitars, and other instruments had been capable of polyphony for centuries, this innovation was new to synthesizers.

Roland introduced its first polyphonic synthesizer, the Jupiter-4, in 1978. The polyphonic sound of the instrument is described on the Vintage Synth Explorer website as "4 individual voices which could be synced together for one fat monophonic lead . . . a nice analog synth for creating weird trippy . . . sounds."[69] With its rich, complex, polyphonic sound, the Jupiter-4 was put to work by almost every pop hit maker of the era, appearing on albums by Stevie Wonder, Michael Jackson, David Bowie, Devo, and Depeche Mode.

Going Digital

Synthesizer technology took another leap forward in 1983 when the Japanese company Yamaha released the DX7, the first commercially successful digital synthesizer, which sold more than 160,000 units. Unlike an analog synthesizer, where sounds were programmed by the player, the digital DX7 used sound-generating software running on a digital microprocessor to create an array of sounds. The musical sounds, or voices, generated by the instrument could be edited, new ones could be created, and all could be stored in a memory bank.

The distinctive metallic sound of the DX7 was recognized as a clearer, brighter alternative to analog synthesizers. Dozens of top-selling musicians, eager to find new sounds, added the DX7 to their records. The sharp, popping licks made possible by the instrument could be heard on New Wave records by the Talking Heads, Brian Eno,

The Yamaha DX7, released in 1983, was the first digital synthesizer to be commercially available. The launch was a great success, and the instrument defined much of the musical movements of the 1980s and 1990s.

and The Cure. With an excellent ability to mimic electric piano and organ sounds, pop artists including Elton John, U2, Queen, Phil Collins, and Steve Winwood prominently featured the DX7 on their hit songs. The instrument was used to create dreamy ambiance on the New Age records of Enya, clanking beats on the hip hop of the Beastie Boys, and smooth, soaring licks on jazz albums by Chick Corea and Herbie Hancock.

The DX7, along with other digital synthesizers, spawned a new genre of music called synthpop. British groups such as A Flock of Seagulls, Thompson Twins, and Duran Duran deemphasized guitars, which had been common on pop records for decades. The bands created droning synthesizer-driven sounds that sounded futuristic and cerebral. The synthpop band Depeche Mode remained popular well into the twenty-first century and sold more than 100 million records worldwide by 2011.

Digital Controllers

The DX7 was actually a keyboard attached to a simplified computer that ran sound-generating software. By the late 1980s similar software programs could be installed on desktop computers that could be used to generate music. While computer music could be made by tapping it out on a typewriter keyboard, best results were achieved with a piano-style keyboard.

When a piano-style keyboard is used to play music on a computer, the keyboard is called a digital controller. Different keys of the controller can be programmed to control a variety of devices. For example, the lower keys might control a drum machine, the middle register might work with a synthesizer to generate violin sounds, and the upper keys might be assigned to play flute. Keyboard controllers also have multiple knobs and sliders, which can manipulate sounds, waver the pitch, add echo, or change the octave.

With a keyboard controller, a single musician can create music using a number of sound generators. These include computers with audio software, racks of boxes that synthesize musical sounds, drum machines, and recording equipment called music sequencers. Controllers can also be used to program lights and stage effects. For example, a keyboardist can trigger a bank of red lights every time he plays a G chord and a bank of blue lights and a smoke machine when he plays a D chord.

The combination of keyboard controllers and powerful personal computers changed the way music was recorded. With simple keyboard controllers, individuals could record multiple tracks of melody, rhythm, and chords, store each track in a sequencer, and alter sounds to imitate a wide variety of acoustic instruments.

A Variety of Controllers

Keyboards that are played with hands are only one type of digital controller. There are also pedal keyboards that serve the same purpose as those on old pipe organs, allowing players to hit bass notes with their feet. Other controllers are made to manage a specific family of instruments, such as the winds or strings, and single instruments such as the guitar and drums.

Wind controllers most often look like plastic clarinets and are used by musicians who wish to mimic the expressive sounds of acoustic wind instruments. Electronic wind controllers have touch-sensitive keys and an air-pressure mechanism that measures the strength of the breath blown into it. The wind controller is connected to a synthesizer, which allows musicians to mimic sounds that include the flute, clarinet, saxophone, oboe, bassoon, trombone, and trumpet.

Guitar controllers, such as those used in the video games Rock Band and Guitar Hero, are operated by pushing buttons on the neck. Because they lack strings and only create pre-programmed sounds, guitar controllers are much more limited than traditional guitars. This is also true with violin and standup bass controllers, which, because of their musical limitations, were never fully embraced by professional musicians. However, electric guitars and other string instruments with pickups can be played through guitar synthesizers. These devices make the notes of the guitar sound like a trumpet, saxophone, piano, organ, or other instrument.

A teen plays an electronic drum set, which can create an endless combination of sounds by transmitting electrical signals to a synthesizer.

Electronic Drums

While guitar controllers and synthesizers have seen limited use, the same cannot be said for electronic drums, which are now nearly as popular as keyboard controllers. Electronic drums are played like acoustic drums and imitate the sounds of traditional drum kits. These are not to be confused with drum machines, which are programmable synthesizers encased in a box and controlled with buttons and knobs. Electronic drums consist of a set of rubber or cloth pads on stands in the same positions as the snare, bass drum, tom toms, hi hat, and cymbals on an acoustic drum kit. The pads are touch-sensitive and when hit with a drumstick send electronic signals to a synthesizer that produces desired sounds.

The first commercially available electronic drum set was produced in 1983 in a basement in Stockholm, Sweden, by Hans Nordelius and Mikael Carlsson. The instrument, known as the Clavia Digital Percussion Plate 1, enabled drummers to hit a rubber disc on top of a small box. The action elicited preprogrammed drum sounds that were stored on a special digital cartridge. By 1984 Clavia was selling the Drum Rack with eight separate rack-mounted drumheads. After Clavia pioneered electronic drums, major manufacturers such as Roland and Yamaha introduced their own kits.

As microprocessors improved over the years, the sounds made by electronic drums became more realistic, and the sets also became cheaper to purchase. In the 2010s starter electronic drum kits cost several hundred dollars, while

Drum Machines

Drum machines were designed to imitate the sounds of snare drums, tom-toms, bass drums, hi-hats, cymbals, and other percussion instruments. The earliest drum machines were analog. They created synthesized percussion sounds that did not sound like real drums but had their own unique tone. The first programmable digital drum machine, the Roland CR-78, released in 1978, allowed users to program and store their own beats. The CR-78 was used extensively to create the repetitive beats heard in dozens of late 1970s disco hits.

Digital drum machines were first introduced in the early 1980s. Rather than produce synthesized percussion, they used dozens of samples, or prerecorded drum sounds. Digital drum machines were polyphonic, allowing users to play up to twelve sounds at once. The drum tracks could be stored, edited, and treated with sound effects. Digital drum machines such as the Oberheim DMX were extremely popular with hip hop artists and were prominently featured on songs by Run DMC, Davy DMX, LL Cool J, and others.

In the early 2000s drum software programs made standalone drum machines obsolete. Available as apps, the drum software turned smartphones and table computers into the latest version of the drum machine. Whatever the hardware or software in use, thanks to digital drums, the beat goes on in the twenty-first century.

professional sets such as Roland's TD-12S V-Stage cost up to $6,000. Top-of-the-line sets feature metal-base cymbals with rubber surfaces, hi-hats with sophisticated motion sensors, and drum pads with mesh weave heads.

Musical Machines

While drum, wind, and keyboard controllers are based on traditional instruments, an entirely new range of digital machines has been used to create music. These devices, such as samplers and audio processors, do not resemble musical instruments. They are manufactured in a variety of styles, but

Musical Apps

In March 2012 Apple Inc. announced that more than 25 billion software applications, or apps, had been downloaded from the company's App Store since it went online in July 2008. Apple's competitor, Android, sold about half that number. While the most popular apps were games such as Angry Birds, millions of people also downloaded software that allowed them to use their smartphones and tablet computers as self-contained musical instruments. The Beatmaker app allowed users to play drums with their fingers. Virtuoso Piano provided six octaves of sampled sounds from a concert grand piano, letting users play with up to five fingers. One of the most popular apps, GarageBand, came with dozens of virtual software instruments, an audio recording studio, and guitar-specific effects that re-created sounds from a variety of amplifiers, effects boxes, and guitars.

In the 2010s, musical apps have made expensive multi-track recording studios nearly obsolete. Thanks to Beatmaker, GarageBand, and other programs, the power of music has been digitized and made portable. Anyone with a smartphone and a $5 app can re-create the sounds of a music studio with the touch of a finger.

most are small, square black boxes featuring pads, buttons, and digital screens. They depend on microprocessors and software programs to manipulate sounds.

Unlike a synthesizer, which generates unique sounds, a sampler uses snippets of previously recorded sounds, or samples. The sounds can be manipulated, played repeatedly in loops, combined with other samples and synthesized sound effects, or edited in other ways. Samples can be replayed by the sampler itself or triggered by a controller such as a keyboard. Most modern samplers are polyphonic, in that they can play more than one sampled sound at a time.

The first samplers were manufactured in small quantities and extremely expensive due to the high cost of microchips at the time. For example, the Synclavier System, released in 1977, was valued at more than $1 million. Although the Synclavier's use was limited to a few professional recording artists who were able to pay the high cost, the early digital sampler was widely influential among cutting-edge musicians. In the early 1980s, for example, Synclaviers were used to create unique sounds by the pioneering fusion jazz guitarists John McLaughlin and Pat Metheny. The quirky composer Frank Zappa, who wrote complex rock and classical orchestral pieces on the Synclavier in the 1980s, preferred the versatility and accuracy of the instrument over live musicians. According to Zappa, "With the Synclavier, any group of imaginary instruments can be invited to play the most difficult passages . . . with [amazing] accuracy—every time."[70]

Like many other digital devices, the price of samplers dropped drastically in the late 1980s as advances in computer technology led to faster and cheaper microchips. By 1987 companies such as Casio, Roland, and Akai were offering digital samplers for the modern equivalent of around $4,300. The E-mu Emulator III, which was popular with professionals, cost about five times more.

Digital samplers were at the heart of the hip hop music explosion. In the late 1980s samplers allowed rappers to mix snippets of soul, funk, and rock into their beat-heavy sounds. The band N.W.A. was out front on the trend with its 1988 album *Straight Outta Compton*. The title track included samples from "Funky Drummer" by James Brown, "You'll Like It Too" by Funkadelic, "Get Me Back on Time, Engine No. 9" by Wilson Pickett, and one of the most sampled songs of all time, "Amen, Brother" by the Winstons. Other samples on *Straight Outta Compton* were taken from rocker Steve Miller, comedian Richard Pryor, and the vocal group the Pointer Sisters. In the decades since hip hop artists sold hundreds of millions of albums featuring sampling, the technique has come to dominate popular music. In 2012 bestselling artists such as Rihanna and Kanye West used samples on nearly every track.

Synthesized Singing

In the late 2000s the sampling trend was nearly eclipsed by the ubiquitous sound of the Auto-Tune pitch corrector software program, which gives a robotic or "gerbil" quality to the human voice. While the Auto-Tune was popularized by pop, rhythm and blues, and hip hop artists in the early twenty-first century, the sound can be traced back more than seventy years to the vocoder, or voice encoder, invented in 1928.

The earliest vocoder was a 7-foot-tall (2m) machine invented by Bell Labs. The device was originally meant to scramble secret military voice communications so they could not be easily interpreted by enemies. The vocoder was used extensively by the United States in World War II to prevent the Nazis from learning about imminent bombing campaigns. After the war, the vocoder was put to use by presidents who used it to communicate messages to the military.

The vocoder moved from top secret to the studio for the first time in 1968. Carlos used the device on a singing track from *A Clockwork Orange* called "March from A Clockwork Orange." Carlos considered the vocoder to be cutting-edge, but not everyone appreciated the sound of the robotic artificial voice. According to Carlos, people had an "emotional resistance" to the sound: "People at first hated our synthesized singing. I watched good friends who enjoyed my synthesized instrumental sounds turn squirmy. They visibly winced."[71]

Despite the initial resistance, the vocoder created weird sounds that caught the attention of major rock acts. The device was put to extensive use in the 1970s by top-selling bands including Pink Floyd, Styx, and the Electric Light Orchestra. During the 1980s the vocoder box was used on New Age, jazz, synthpop, and rock records.

The Auto-Tune Effect

The vocoder operated by mixing the voice with an audio signal, producing a sound effect that created a muddy, robotic sound. In 1997 Antares Audio Technologies improved on voice encoder technology when it introduced the Auto-Tune audio processor. Auto-Tune was sold as a software program and as a stand-alone, rack-mounted unit. Instead of distorting a vocal signal, Auto-Tune analyzed the frequency of a sung note and manipulated it in various ways. From the outset, the Auto-Tune was used in digital recording studios as a pitch corrector; when the software detected slightly off-key notes, it could shift the pitch slightly to make it sound on key. The processor could also be used to shift the pitch in extreme ways that distorted vocals. This caused notes to waver in a way that made a singer sound robotic.

The Auto-Tune sound effect was first used by the singer Cher on her hit single "Believe" in 1998. The vocal effects on "Believe" feature Cher as a squeaky robot on some of the verses where she sounds more like a synthesizer keyboard than a human singer. The futuristic sound of "Believe" was unique enough that it grabbed the public's attention and sold more than 10 million copies. After "Believe" became one of the bestselling singles of all time, the Auto-Tune sound came to be called the Cher Effect. Pop music

Pop star Cher holds a copy of her CD at a book- and CD-signing event at a New York City bookstore in 1998. The use of auto-tune in her hit song "Believe" sparked widespread use of the voice-altering technology.

The "Gerbil" Effect

Pop music critic Sasha Frere-Jones explains how the Auto-Tune audio processor changes the sound of the human voice:

Most of the time, Auto-Tune is used imperceptibly, to correct flat or sharp notes. . . . Often, it solves logistical problems: an artist has left the studio and has no opportunity to return just to re-sing one or two off notes. But pitch correction has also taken on a second life, as an effect . . . Auto-Tune software detects pitch, and when a vocal is routed through Auto-Tune, and a setting called "retune speed" is set to zero, warbling begins. This, roughly, is what happens: Auto-Tune locates the pitch of a recorded vocal, and moves that recorded information to the nearest "correct" note in a scale, which is selected by the user. With the speed set to zero, unnaturally rapid corrections eliminate *portamento*, the musical term for the slide between two pitches. Portamento is a natural aspect of speaking and singing, central to making people sound like people. . . . Processed at zero speed, Auto-Tune turns the lolling curves of the human voice into a zigzag of right-angled steps. These steps may represent "perfect" pitches, but when sung pitches alternate too quickly the result sounds unnatural, a fluttering that is described by some engineers as "the gerbil" and by others as "robotic."

Sasha Frere-Jones. "The Gerbil's Revenge." *New Yorker*, July 9, 2008. http://www .newyorker.com/arts/critics/musical/2008/06/09/080609crmu_music_frerejones ?currentPage=1.

critic Sasha Frere-Jones explains the Cher Effect: "Auto-Tune can produce a controlled version of losing control, hinting at various histrionic [dramatic] stations of the human voice—crying, sighing, laughing—without troubling the singer."[72]

After the success of "Believe," Auto-Tune became pervasive, heard on albums by Madonna and dancehall hits by Jamaican rappers. No one is more closely associated with Auto-Tune than the rhythm and blues singer Faheem Najm, known as T-Pain. In 2007 T-Pain racked up four Top 10 singles using Auto-Tune. The sound is prominently featured on his top-selling albums *Thr33 Ringz* (2008) and *RevolveR* (2011). T-Pain's Auto-Tune success inspired dozens of other artists, including Snoop Dogg, Lil Wayne, and Kanye West, to incorporate the audio processor into their hit songs.

Not everyone was thrilled with the popularity of Auto-Tune. In 2009 rapper Jay-Z recorded the single "D.O.A. (Death of Auto-Tune)" to criticize the overuse of the effect in pop music. Jay-Z complained that Auto-Tune had become a crutch for those who were not capable of singing on key. Other Auto-Tune critics chastised country artists such as Faith Hill and Shania Twain who used the pitch-correcting device during concert performances to prevent off-key notes from being heard by the audience.

Despite some criticism, voice processors, samplers, and synthesizers have become as important as guitars, drums, pianos, and other acoustic instruments in producing the music of the twenty-first century. Times have changed, and the human ear has adjusted to a new range of sounds blasting from car stereos, cell phones, iPads, video games, and massive home theater speaker systems. Digital instruments tie together the old and the new, re-creating the ancient sounds of the harpsichord and lute along with robot voices and sound effects that rumble, screech, and sometimes soothe.

Introduction: The Sounds of Music

1. Quoted in John Lubbock. "The Pleasures of Life." Authorama, September 2003. http://www.authorama.com/pleasures-of-life-21.html.
2. Quoted in Keith Spence. *Living Music.* New York: Gloucester, 1979, p. 8.

Chapter 1: Percussion

3. Mickey Hart and Jay Stevens. *Drumming at the Edge of Magic.* San Francisco: HarperCollins, 1990, p. 70.
4. Hart and Stevens. *Drumming at the Edge of Magic,* p. 34.
5. Töm Klöwer. *The Joy of Drumming.* Diever, Holland: Binkey Kok, 1997, p. 68.
6. Bernard S. Mason. *Drums, Tomtoms and Rattles.* New York: Dover, 1974, p. 171.
7. James Blades. *Percussion Instruments and Their History.* London: Faber and Faber, 1974, pp. 37–38.
8. Charles L. White. *Drums Through the Ages.* Los Angeles: Sterling, 1960, p. 64.
9. Blades. *Percussion Instruments and Their History,* p. 45.
10. Hart and Stevens. *Drumming at the Edge of Magic,* p. 38.
11. Layne Redmond. *When the Drummers Were Women.* New York: Three Rivers, 1997, p. 19.
12. Blades. *Percussion Instruments and Their History,* p. 51.
13. White. *Drums Through the Ages,* pp. 140–141.
14. White. *Drums Through the Ages,* p. 147.
15. Hart and Stevens. *Drumming at the Edge of Magic,* p. 61.
16. Hart and Stevens. *Drumming at the Edge of Magic,* p. 18.

Chapter 2: Woodwinds

17. Raymond Meylan. *The Flute.* London: B.T. Batsford, 1988, p. 13.
18. James Galway. *Flute.* New York: Schirmer, 1982, pp. 18–19.
19. Quoted in Galway. *Flute,* p. 22.
20. Quoted in Meylan. *The Flute,* p. 114.
21. Meylan. *The Flute,* p. 112.
22. Quoted in Nancy Toff. *The Development of the Modern Flute.* New York: Taplinger, 1979, pp. 71–72.
23. Anthony Baines. *Woodwind Instruments and Their History.* New York: Dover, 1991, p. 76.

24. Quoted in Gunther Joppig. *The Oboe and the Bassoon.* Portland, OR: Amadeus, 1988, p. 18.
25. Quoted in Joppig. *The Oboe and the Bassoon,* p. 21.
26. Baines. *Woodwind Instruments and Their History,* p. 268.
27. Baines. *Woodwind Instruments and Their History,* pp. 277–279.
28. Baines. *Woodwind Instruments and Their History,* p. 287.
29. Jack Brymer. *Clarinet.* New York: Schirmer, 1976, p. 9.
30. Quoted in Brymer. *Clarinet,* p. 29.
31. Baines. *Woodwind Instruments and Their History,* p. 331.
32. Quoted in Richard Ingham. *The Cambridge Companion to the Saxophone.* Cambridge, England: Cambridge University Press, 1998, p. 16.
33. Quoted in Anthony Baines. *Brass Instruments: Their History and Development.* New York: Charles Scribner's Sons, 1978, pp. 254–255.
34. Galway. *Flute,* pp. 1–2.

Chapter 3: Brass

35. Trevor Herbert and John Wallace (eds). *The Cambridge Companion to Brass Instruments.* Cambridge, England: Cambridge University Press, 1997, p. 1.
36. Quoted in Herbert and Wallace. *The Cambridge Companion to Brass Instruments,* p. 19.
37. Edward Tarr. *The Trumpet.* London: B.T. Batsford, 1988, p. 19.
38. Quoted in Curt Sachs. *The History of Musical Instruments.* Mineola, NY: Dover, 2006, p. 100.
39. Quoted in Tarr. *The Trumpet,* p. 20.
40. Quoted in Herbert and Wallace. *The Cambridge Companion to Brass Instruments,* p. 43.
41. Quoted in Tarr. *The Trumpet,* p. 61.
42. Quoted in Herbert and Wallace. *The Cambridge Companion to Brass Instruments,* p. 50.
43. Herbert and Wallace. *The Cambridge Companion to Brass Instruments,* pp. 56–57.
44. Quoted in Ian Lovett. "'Tuba Raids' Plague Schools in California." *New York Times,* February 9, 2012. http://www.nytimes.com/2012/02/10/education/tuba-thefts-plague-california-schools.html.
45. Sam Quinones. "Tubas Become Horns of Plenty." *Los Angeles Times,* November 15, 2011. http://articles.latimes.com/2011/nov/15/local/la-me-tuba-20111115.

Chapter 4: Strings

46. Frederic V. Grunfeld. *The Art and Times of the Guitar.* London: Macmillan, 1969, p. 41.
47. Robert Ruadh. "Gaelic Harps and Harpers in Ireland and Scotland." 2012. http://www.silcom.com/~vikman/isles/scriptorium/harps/harps.html.
48. Grunfeld. *The Art and Times of the Guitar,* p. 45.
49. Quoted in Grunfeld. *The Art and Times of the Guitar,* p. 55.

50. Quoted in Hortense Panum. *The Stringed Instruments of the Middle Ages.* New York: Da Capo, 1971, p. 410.

51. Panum. *The Stringed Instruments of the Middle Ages*, p. 423.

52. Tony Bacon. *The Ultimate Guitar Book.* London: Dorling Kindersley, 1991, p. 8.

53. Quoted in Grunfeld. *The Art and Times of the Guitar*, p. 109.

54. Quoted in Grunfeld. *The Art and Times of the Guitar*, p. 235.

Chapter 5: Keyboards

55. C.F. Abdy Williams. *The Story of the Organ.* Detroit: Singing Tree, 1972, pp. 3–4.

56. Bernard Sonnaillon. *King of Instruments.* New York: Rizzoli, 1984, p. 29.

57. Nicholas Thistlewaite and Geoffrey Webber (eds). *The Cambridge Companion to the Organ.* Cambridge, England: Cambridge University Press, 1997, p. 8.

58. Quoted in Hans T. David and Arthur Mendel (eds). *The Bach Reader.* New York: W.W. Norton, 1966, p. 236.

59. David Crombie. *Piano.* San Francisco: GPI, 1995, p. 11.

60. Crombie. *Piano*, p. 4.

61. Quoted in David Rowland (ed). *The Cambridge Companion to the Piano.* Cambridge, England: Cambridge University Press, 1998, p. 17.

62. Quoted in Rowland. *The Cambridge Companion to the Piano*, p. 22.

63. Rowland. *The Cambridge Companion to the Piano*, p. 27.

64. Crombie. *Piano*, p. 33.

Chapter 6: Digital Instruments

65. Quoted in David Henderson. *Journey to a Plugged In State of Mind.* London: Cherry Red, 2010, p. 40.

66. Geoffrey Stanton. *The Digital Musician.* Colfax, NC: Wayne Leupold Editions, 2009, p. 10.

67. Quoted in "Strange Days." *Rolling Stone*, 2012. www.rollingstone .com/music/song-stories/strange -days-the-doors.

68. Bruce Elder. "Switched-On Bach." AllMusic, 2012. http://www.allmu sic.com/album/switched-on-bach -r255332/review.

69. "Roland Jupiter-4." Vintage Synth Explorer, 2012. www.vintagesynth .com/roland/jup4.php.

70. Frank Zappa and Peter Occhiogrosso. *The Real Frank Zappa Book.* New York: Poseidon, 1989, pp. 172–173.

71. Quoted in Dave Tompkins. *How to Wreck a Nice Beach.* Chicago: Stop Smiling Media, 2010, p. 165.

72. Sasha Frere-Jones. "The Gerbil's Revenge." *New Yorker*, July 9, 2008. http://www.newyorker.com/arts /critics/musical/2008/06/09 /080609crmu_music_frerejones ?currentPage=1.

Academy of St. Martin in the Fields

Mozart: Concertos for Flute and Harp, 2004

Louis Armstrong

The Best of the Hot 5 and Hot 7 Recordings, 2002

Armstrong's brassy cornet and trumpet sound on this collection of songs was new, complex, and rich. No one had ever before heard anything like it. The hot bands are prime examples of the New Orleans jazz sound.

The Beatles

Sgt. Pepper's Lonely Hearts Club Band, 1967

The Beatles popularized the use of orchestral instruments in rock music. Different tracks in this album feature harpsichords, harps, saxophones, trombones, a string quartet, and an orchestra.

William Bennett and Nicholas Daniel et al.

French Chamber Music for Woodwinds, 1994

Berliner Philharmoniker

Bizet: L'Arlésienne Suites Nos. 1 and2, Carmen Suite, 1985

The Magic Flute, 2010

Mozart's magical opera features the enchanting sounds of flutes, which helped solidify the role of the instrument in the symphony orchestra.

Chuck Berry

The Chess Box, 1988

Rock-and-roll guitar was never the same after rock's poet laureate ripped out the hot licks on 1950s classics such as "Johnny B. Goode," "Maybellene," and "Rock and Roll Music," setting the standard for all who would follow.

Boston Symphony Orchestra

Ravel: Bolero, 1987

This one-movement orchestral piece, composed by Maurice Ravel in 1928, was one of the first large ensemble pieces to employ saxophones. The piece also makes fine use of bassoons, clarinets, trombones, tubas, and other orchestral instruments.

Wendy Carlos

Switched-On Bach, 2001

This album, first released in 1968, proved the Moog Synthesizer was not just a gimmick. Using the primitive, monophonic synthesizer, Carlos spent months assembling tracks and over-dubs to create the final product, which sold more than half a million copies and popularized classical music performances on synthesizers.

Celtic Harp Soundscapes

Celtic Harp and Traditional Irish Music, 2010

Charlie Christian

The Genius of the Electric Guitar, 1987

Christian, one of the first players to use the electric guitar in jazz, shines on this four-CD compilation, recorded with such greats as Benny Goodman, Lionel Hampton, Gene Krupa, Cootie Williams, and Lester Young. The re-mastered tracks from the late 1930s and early 1940s sound crisp and clean.

Johnny Conga

Breaking Skin/Rompiendo el Cuero, 2009

Los Cuates de Sinaloa

Pegando Con Tuba, 2009

Tooting, churning tuba licks interweave with the accordion on these Mexican banda songs. The traditional sound, has become increasingly popular in Southern California.

Miles Davis

The Complete Birth of the Cool, 1998

These historic recordings, released in 1957, provide an essential introduction to Davis and the cool sound he pioneered with his flugelhorn.

Niklas Eklund, Nils-Erik Sparf, and the Drottningholm Baroque Ensemble

The Art of the Baroque Trumpet, Vol. 1, 1995

Duke Ellington

The Cotton Club Days 1926–1938, 2012

The father of sophisticated jazz presents swinging clarinets, tootling trumpets, red-hot trombones, and stomping drums. Songs such as "Doin' the Frog," "Harmony in Harlem," and "The Gal from Joe's" are played by some of the best big band virtuosos ever assembled.

James Galway

Celebrating 70—A Collection of Personal Favorites, 2009

On this compilation, the renowned Irish flautist shows off his skills on folk songs, movie scores, classical music, and jazz jams with renowned pianist Claude Bolling.

Benny Goodman

The Essential Benny Goodman, 2007

Few artists played the "licorice stick" as well as Goodman, and this record contains forty classic swing performances including "Bugle Call Rag," "Get Happy," and "Swingtime in the Rockies" presented in a big band setting with brass, percussion, keyboard, and woodwind virtuosos.

Mickey Hart

Planet Drum, 1991

This all-percussion workout by the respected drummer from the Grateful Dead features extended percussion grooves with echoes of ancient tribal polyrhythms mixed with modern psychedelic drum jams.

Jimi Hendrix

Axis: Bold as Love, 1967

Electric Ladyland, 1968

On songs such as ". . . And the Gods Made Love," "1983," and the classic "All Along the Watchtower," the visionary guitarist demonstrates a wizardry on the guitar and mastery of electronic effects that has been imitated by many but surpassed by none.

Christopher Herrick

Bach: The Complete Organ Music, 2002

Johann Sebastian Bach wrote hundreds of sonatas, fugues, concertos, and other pieces for the organ, and renowned British organist Herrick has assembled 362 of those songs for this ambitious compilation of beautiful and inspiring music.

David Hill

Winchester Cathedral Organ Spectacular, 2010

This album features the works of Bach, Felix Mendelssohn, Claude Debussy, and others played on the famous pipe organ at Winchester Cathedral in England.

Joji Hirota and Hiten Ryu Daiko

Japanese Drums, 2010

Scott Joplin

Ragtime (The Music of Scott Joplin), 2006

Joplin forever changed the sound of music and laid the groundwork for jazz, jump blues, rhythm and blues, and rock with these amazing keyboard compositions, which include "Maple Leaf Rag," "The Entertainer," and "Stoptime Rag."

Louis Jordan

Let the Good Times Roll—The Anthology 1938–1953, 2008

Saxophonist, songwriter, and arranger Jordan rewrote the sounds of music and laid the foundations for rock and roll with the jump blues and boogie-woogie tunes on this double-CD set. Classics such as "Saxa-Woogie," "Five Guys Named Moe," and "Choo Choo Ch'Boogie" showcase wailing saxophones, thumping doghouse bass, pounding piano, and jumping percussion.

Koto

Koto, 2011

This collection showcases traditional music for the Japanese koto harp.

Andrei Krylov

Lute and Guitar Music of Renaissance Holland, Germany, England, France, Italy, Spain, 1998

Michael Levy

An Ancient Lyre, 2009

Levy revives the sound of the lyre, playing music interpreted from ancient fragments of musical nations discovered in India, Mesopotamia, Egypt, and Greece.

Franz Liszt

Liszt Complete Piano Music, Vol. 17, Schubert Song Transcriptions 2, 2001

Little Richard

Here's Little Richard, 1957

London Philharmonic Orchestra and Choir

Handel: The Messiah, 2002

The London Philharmonic performs a stirring illustration of the symphonic sound produced by orchestral instruments. The crescendo of "Hallelujah Chorus" provides a stunning example of the power and glory of the timpani.

London Philharmonic Orchestra and Nicholas Braithwaite

British Horn Concertos, 2007

Wynton Marsalis

Wynton Marsalis Plays Handel, Purcell, Torelli, Fasch, and Molter, 1984

Widely known as one of the premier promoters of jazz, trumpeter Marsalis shows he can also hold his own with a symphony orchestra as he soars through a variety of graceful trumpet pieces written in the seventeenth and eighteenth centuries.

Harpo Marx

The Best Of, 2010

Although he is best remembered as the comical Marx Brother who wore a curly wig, honked a bicycle horn, and never spoke, Harpo was one of the great harpists of the twentieth century, and the jazz, pop, and even boogie-woogie sounds on this album demonstrate his skill.

Freddie Mitchell and Hen Gates

Rockin' Wailin' Saxophone, 2010

These sax supermen get down and dirty, delivering gutty sax solos on slow rhythm and blues songs, blues, rock and roll, and jumping jazz.

Thelonious Monk

Complete Blue Note Recordings, 1994

On these four discs, recorded between 1947 and 1952, Monk shows off his quirky improvisational piano style and songwriting chops. Signature compositions include "Ruby My Dear," "Misterioso," and "Straight No Chaser."

Bill Monroe and His Blue Grass Boys

Bill Monroe: Anthology, 2003

Fifty hits recorded by the father of bluegrass music over two decades provide stunning examples of the fiddle, guitar, banjo, and mandolin played by virtuosos including Vassar Clements, Peter Rowan, Earl Scruggs, and Monroe.

Jelly Roll Morton

The Complete Library of Congress Recordings, 2005

National Percussion Group of Kenya

Roots!!—African Drums, 1989

The rich and varied sounds of traditional African drumming are featured on this record with percussion resembling bird and animal calls, rhythms used during women's ceremonial dances, and beats played by shamans during rituals.

Paul O'Dette

Bach Lute Works, Vol. 1, 2007

Ernst Ottensamer and Johannes Wildner et al.

Mozart: Bassoon Concerto, Oboe Concerto, Clarinet Concerto, 1990

Few composers wrote as skillfully as Mozart and fewer still were able to conceive music that so beautifully accentuated the versatility and tonal qualities of the single- and double-reed woodwinds.

Petros Tabouris Ensemble

Ancient Greek Musical Instruments— Music of Ancient Greece, 2009

Preservation Hall Jazz Band

The Essential Preservation Hall Jazz Band, 2007

This group, formed in New Orleans in 1961, plays music with roots that stretch back to eighteenth-century French society dances, nineteenth-century military parades, and twentieth-century street corner jazz ensembles. Few bands utilize the clarinet, trombone, trumpet, and tuba to such delightful ends.

Tito Puente

Top Percussion, 1992

Tito Puente, known as the "King of Latin Music," was one of the world's greatest percussionists, and he played jazz, cha cha, salsa, and mambo to millions during his legendary fifty-year career. On this album, Puente pays homage to the spiritual roots of Latin music by laying down pure West African rhythms alongside tribal chants. A few sizzling tracks feature Willie Bobo wailing on the timbales.

Purdue University "All-American" Marching Band

College Fight Songs—Purdue Boilermakers, 2005

Django Reinhardt, Stéphane Grappelli and the Quintet of the Hot Club of France

Parisian Swing, 1999

Few musicians could coax as much sound out of the guitar and fiddle than Django Reinhardt and Stéphane Grappelli. On this remastered album with fifty-one songs, the hot licks exchanged by the two men bring back the golden age of Paris in the 1930s.

Earl Scruggs

The Essential Earl Scruggs, 1980

The Jimi Hendrix of the banjo can be heard on these forty songs defining the very sound of bluegrass with his hot picked licks backed by Bill Monroe, Lester Flatt, the Nitty Gritty Dirt Band, the Earl Scruggs Revue, and others.

The Skillet Lickers

Old-Time Fiddle Tunes and Songs from North Georgia, 2007

Tater Tate and Red Smiley and the Bluegrass Cutups

Fiddle and Banjo Instrumentals: Bluegrass and Old Timey Tunes, 2009

Richard Troeger

Johann Sebastian Bach: The Six Partitas, Bach on Clavichord, 1999

United States Marine Band

Sousa's Greatest Hits and Some That Should Have Been, 1999

John Philip Sousa's military marches provided a source of inspiration for early New Orleans jazz bands while showing off the musical versatility of brass, woodwinds, and percussion. This album features the oldest, and some would say best, military band in the United States playing Sousa classics.

Various Artists

Classical Harp Music, 2008

The Gringo Guide to Salsa, 2006

The fourteen songs on this compilation feature an array of percussion instruments and drums in the hands of some of the greatest Latin percussionists of the modern age.

Instrumental Music of the 1600s (Music by Gabrieli, Morley, Holborne, Scheidt and Others), 2004

The Jazz Woodwinds Collection, 1995

Phil Woods, Eddie Daniels, and others jam on some jazz classics while showing off the rich, mellow, and versatile tones of flutes, clarinets, and other woodwinds.

Samba Percussion Live in Concert, 2000

The Very Best of Andean Flutes, 2006

Violin Masterworks, 2009

This set of 486 songs contains concertos, sonatas, partitas, and more written by Johann Sebastian Bach, Ludwig van Beethoven, Wolfgang Amedeus Mozart, Maurice Ravel, Antonio Vivaldi, and others. The classic sound of the violin can be heard with harps, pianos, string quartets, and full orchestras.

Muddy Waters

The Chess 50th Anniversary Collection: Muddy Waters—His Best, 1947–1955, 1997

Muddy Waters made his first guitar with a stick, a cigar box, and some wire. By the time these songs were recorded, he was the king of Delta blues slide guitar, creating music that influenced generations of rock, blues, and jazz guitarists.

Bob Wills and His Texas Playboys

For the Last Time, 1994

The sound of western swing is exemplified with steel guitar licks by Leon McAuliffe and fiddle by Johnny Gimble.

Stevie Wonder

Talking Book, 1972

Wonder's prodigious use of the electric clavinet on songs such as "Superstition" and "Higher Ground" made the updated version of the medieval clavichord a staple of the funk music sound of the 1970s.

aerophone: Any musical instrument in which the sound is produced by air being blown into it. Common aerophones include woodwinds such as the flute and clarinet and brass instruments such as the trumpet and French horn.

analog: An analog signal is a sound directly from the source, be it a person playing a guitar or a singer with a microphone creating a vocal track directly on recording tape. An analog signal is the opposite of a digital signal, where a sound is broken down into binary code stored on a computer.

arpeggio: The series of notes in a chord played in sequence.

chordophone: Any stringed instrument from which sound is produced by vibrating strings stretched between two points.

digital controller: A keyboard, electronic drum set, or other device used to play music on a computer.

fret: A ridge on the fingerboard of a stringed instrument that divides the neck into segments related to musical intervals.

gut: A natural fiber found in the intestines of cows or sheep wound tightly and used as instrument strings; sometimes referred to as catgut, although cats were never used for this purpose.

idiophone: A percussion instrument made from resonating material that does not have to be tuned.

membranophones: Drums that produce sound when the drumhead made from an animal skin, or membrane, is struck.

microprocessor: A programmable integrated circuit that functions as a computer's central processing unit (CPU). Microprocessors perform functions such as computation, text editing, multimedia display, communications, and producing and recording music.

octave: An eight-note interval between two notes of the same name, represented by "Do" in the Do Re Mi Fa So La Ti Do system of singing musical scales.

overtone: A note that is higher than the fundamental note. Horn players hit overtones by tightening their lips to produce higher notes.

plectrum: A pick used to pluck or strum a stringed instrument. Plectra include guitar picks, finger picks, and feather quills that pluck each string on a harpsichord.

polyphonic: Music with several notes or melodies sounding at once.

reed: A small piece of reed cane, fixed to the mouthpiece of a woodwind instrument, which vibrates to produce sound.

soukous: A highly rhythmic style of dance music that originated in Congo and spread across most of Africa. Soukous bands often feature several kit drummers, hand drummers, and percussionists.

FOR MORE INFORMATION

Books

Tony Bacon. *2000 Guitars*. San Diego: Thunder Bay, 2009. Guitars of every age, style, model, and manufacture are on display in this book, which showcases the instrument in chapters that include acoustic, solid body, bass, hollow body, and more.

Hugh Benham. *Baroque Music in Focus*. London: Rhinegold, 2010. This book provides a comprehensive look at musical works of the Baroque era as well as in-depth examinations of the lives and careers of the two greatest Baroque composers: Johann Sebastian Bach and George Frideric Handel.

Mickey Hart and Jay Stevens. *Drumming at the Edge of Magic*. San Francisco: HarperCollins, 1990. The man who played drums for the Grateful Dead for more than thirty years shares the compelling story of percussion, drums, and drumming.

Ananda Mitra. *Digital Music: Computers That Make Music*. New York: Chelsea House, 2010. This book provides an exploration of modern digital music and how it is composed and played on PCs, laptops, tablet computers, smartphones, and MP3 players.

Ruth Thomson. *Musical Instruments*. London: Franklin Watts, 2011. This book describes how a variety of instruments from around the world are made, explains how to play them, and also includes step-by-step instructions on how to make six traditional musical instruments.

Susan VanHecke. *Raggin' Jazzin' Rockin': A History of American Musical Instrument Makers*. Honesdale, PA: Boyds Mills, 2011. This book explores the fascinating accomplishments of U.S. inventors and innovators such as Leo Fender, Laurens Hammond, and Bob Moog, who made musical instrument history.

Websites

AllMusic (www.allmusic.com). Originally known as All Music Guide (AMG), the AllMusic website is one of the most comprehensive music guides on the Internet. The site has in-depth information about recorded music throughout the decades as well as the latest hits and descriptions of genres from opera to punk.

Drum! (www.drummagazine.com). The motto of *Drum!* magazine is "Drumming for Fanatics." The online version features enthusiastic drum articles, news, equipment and music reviews, lesson videos, and a special site for hand drummers.

Electronic Musician (www.emusician .com). This online magazine is dedicated to those who play, perform, and record digital music. The site features equipment reviews, artist biographies, lessons, tips, and the latest news concerning computerized music making.

Guitar Site (www.guitarsite.com). This e-zine is dedicated to guitars and guitar players with band bios, discussion forums, and countless links to musical styles and players.

Modern Drummer (www.moderndrum mer.com). The online version of *Modern Drummer* features an A-to-Z listing of professional drummers with related articles, interviews, and equipment and music reviews. The site also provides news, educational material, and an endless stream of information about drums and drummers.

Oddmusic (www.oddmusic.com). This site is home to unique musical instruments. The Gallery section features information about traditional instruments such as the balalaika and kava as well as cutting-edge hybrid musical instruments such as the bamboo saxophone and the elemento.

Films

Les Paul: Chasing Sound, 2007
Les Paul stars in this film about the electric guitar that bears his name. Footage includes interviews with superstar guitarists such as B.B. King and Merle Haggard as well as clips of the Beatles, the Who, and others using his innovative instrument.

Moog, 2004
This documentary about Robert Moog, inventor of the modern synthesizer, portrays his collaborations with other musicians over the years and features Moog's ideas about creativity, design, music, and technology.

Note By Note, 2009
This film follows the complex construction of a Steinway piano, a twelve-month process that involves more than 450 craftsmen, 12,000 individual parts, and countless hours of fine-tuned labor by a dying breed of skilled cabinet makers, tuners, and other hand-crafters.

A

Aerophones, 26, 44
Armstrong, Louis, 39, 52, *52*, 55
Auto-Tune, 114–117

B

Babbitt, Milton, 101–102
Bach, Johann Sebastian, 21, 51, 53, 68, 88, 93, 101
Bagpipes, 33, 84
Banda, 59
Banjos, 62, 77, 78–79
Bass drums, 9, 23, 24, 110–111
Bass stringed instruments, 71, 73–74, 80–82, 106
Bassoons, 26, 36-37
Beatles, 57, 104–105
Beethoven, Ludwig van, 7–8, 29, 56, 65, 99, 106
Bell Labs, 114
Bells, 9, 12–13, 23
Bluegrass music, 72, 73
Blues music, 22, 42, 79
Blühmel, Friedrich, 53
Boehm, Theobald, 29–30, 35, 38
Bone whistles, 27–28
Brass instruments, *45, 49, 52, 57*
    materials, 46–49, 54
    military music and, 55
    overview, 44–47
    religion and, 47, 48, 49
    See also specific instruments

Bugles, 54–55

C

Carlos, Wendy, 105–106, 114
Cellos, 62, 71, 106
Chalumeau, 37
Cher, 115–116, *115*
Chordophones, 60–62, *61*, 74
Christian, Charlie, 79
Clarinets, 26, 37–39, *38*, 106
Classical music
    brass instruments and, 53, 56
    percussion instruments and, 7, 15, 21, 22
    woodwinds and, 29, 37–38
Clavichords, 89, 92
Clay drums, 18
Congas, 18–20
Contrabasses, 71, 73
Contrabassoons, 36
Contrapuntal music, 92–93, 97
Cornets, 40, 52, 55
Cornetts, 53, 54
Cowbells, 12, 23
Cream (band), 82
Cristofori, Bartolomeo, 94–95, 99
Cymbals, *14*, 23–24, 111

D

Dance, 10–11, 72, *75*
Davis, Miles, 41, 55
Denner, Johann Christoph, 37

Dodds, Warren "Baby," 23
Doors, The (band), 104–105
Double basses, 71
Double bassoons, 36
Drum machines, 110–112
Drum Rack, 111
Drums, *17, 22*
   banjos and, 77
   drum sets, 22–24
   foot pedals, 23–24
   harps and, 64
   military uses, 19, 21
   rhythm and, 9
   shapes, 17
   See also Percussion, *specific instruments*
Dulcimers, 62, 90–91

E

Electric basses, 80–82
Electric drums, 110–112

F

Fender instruments, *79,* 80, 81, 100
Flugelhorns, 54–55
Flutes, 27–30, 35, 106
Folk music, 71–72
Frame drums, 18
French horns, 44, 56–57, *57*

G

Galway, James, 29, 42
Gibson guitars, 72, 80, 81
Gongs, 14–15, 25
Gospel music, 73, 74
Guitars, *75, 79*
   development, 74–76, 78–79
   electric, 79–82
   Latin, 76
   lute and, 68
   Moorish, 76

   popularity, 72
   steel, 78
   synthesizers and, 106
Gut strings, 61, 62, 90

H

Hammond organs, 89, 100
Handel, George Frideric, 21–22, 51
Harps, 62–66, *66,* 104
Harpsichords, 83, 92–97, *92,* 106
Haydn, Franz Joseph, 7, 56, 65, 71
Hebenstreit, Pantaleon, 90
Hendrix, Jimi, *79,* 80
Hi-hats, 23–24
Hip hop, 113–114, 117

I

Idiophones, 10–11, *11*

J

Jazz
   brass instruments and, 52, 53, 55, 58
   conga and, 20
   drum sets and, 22–24
   free-form, 42
   improvisation, 99
   invention, 22
   strings and, 74, 79
   woodwinds and, 38–40, 42
Joplin, Scott, 99
Jordan, Louis, 42, *42*

K

Kettledrums, 20–22
Keyboards, *87, 92*
   dampers, 96
   definition, 83
   mufflers, 96
   pedals, 83, 85, 87–89, 96, 109

rubato and, 97
stops, 85–86, 94
See also specific instruments
Koto, 62, 90, *91*

L

Liszt, Franz, 89, *97*, 98
Lutes, 34, 66–69, 71, 72, 76, 104
Lyres, 62–63

M

Mandolins, 62, 68, 72
Marx, Harpo, 65–66
Megaphones, 47
Membranophones, 17, *17*
Military music, 19, 21, 33, 35, 39, 40, 55
Minimoog, 105, 106
Minstrels, 33, 77
Monk, Thelonious, 99
Monteverdi, Claudio, 71
Moog synthesizers, 102–106, *102*
Morton, Jelly Roll, 39, 99
Mozart, Wolfgang Amadeus, 7, 37, 56, 65,
    71, 96–97

N

New Wave music, 107–108

O

Oblique flutes, 28
Oboes, 26, 31–36
Oliver, King, 39, 52
Opera, 40, 53, 55–56, 58, 65, 71
Organs (musical instrument), 83–89, *87*,
    95, 100

P

Parker, Charlie, 42

Pedals
    digital instruments and, 109
    drum pedals, 22–24
    guitar pedals, 78
    harp pedals, 65
    keyboard pedals, 83, 85, 87–89, 96, 109
Percussion
    military uses, 19, 21
    overview, 9
    religion and, 10, 12, 13–14, *14*, 16
    rhythm and, 9–12, 14, 20–25
    telegraphing messages and, 15–16
    See also Drums
Pianos, 36, 83, 94–99, 100, 106
Piccolo trumpets, 53
Pickup (device), 78, 79, 80, 100–101
Pitch, definition, 26–27
Plectrums, 92, 93–94
Polymoog, 106
Pommers, 33–36
Psaltery, 62, 89, 90

Q

Quills, 92, 93, 94

R

Ragtime, 22, 98–99
Rattles, 9, 13–14, 25
RCA Laboratories, 101
Recorders (musical instrument), 26
Reed instruments, 30–42
Reeds, 26
Rhythm, 9–12, 14, 20–25, 58–61, 73–75,
    79, 109
Rhythm and blues, 20, 24, 74, 89, 114
Rickenbacker company, 79, 81
Rock and roll
    bells and, 12
    brass instruments and, 53
    drums and, 20, 24–25
    electric guitars and, 41

gongs and, 15
Hammond organs and, 100
saxophones and, 41
standup basses and, 73–74
strings and, 41, 73–74, 82
synthesizers and, 104–105
Roland instruments, 106–107, 112, 113
Rossini, Gioachino, 40, 65, 106

S

Salsa music, 12, 20
Samba, 12
Samplers, 112–114
Sax, Adolphe, 38, 40
Saxophones, 26, 38, 40–41, 106
Shamans, 10, 47
Shawms, 33–36, 50
Sitars, 62, 104
Slaves, 77, 84, 85
Sleigh bells, 13
Slide trumpets, 50–51, 55
Slit drums, 15–17
Snare drums, 22–23
Sound boxes, 64, 65
Soundboards, 62, 67, 74, 89, 92
Spalding, Esperanza, 73, 74
Standup basses, 73–74, 80, 109
Stradivari, Antonio, 71
String quartets, 71
Strings
    drums and, 64
    materials, 60–62, 67–69, 90, 92
    overview, 60–62
    pickups and, 79
    See also specific instruments
Subcontrabass, 58
Swing music, 39, 42, 79
Symphony orchestras, 15, 21, 37–38
Synclavier System, 113
Syncopated music, 98
Synthesized singing, 114–117
Synthesizers, 101–117, 102

T

Tablature, 76
Tambourines, 18
Tambours, 21
Timpanis, 20–22, 22
Tom-toms, 20, 23,111
Trombones, 45, 55–56, 106
Trumpets, 35, 45–55, 49, 84
Tubas, 49, 58–59, 106

U

Ukuleles, 72
Upright basses, 71

V

Video games, 109
Violas, 70, 71
Violins, 35, 61, 68, 69–73, 70, 106
Vocoders, 114–115

W

Wagner, Richard, 37, 58
Walberg, Barney, 23
Woodblocks, 10, 23
Woodwinds
    materials, 26–33, 36, 38
    military music and, 33, 35, 39, 40
    organic music and, 43
    overview, 26–27
    pitch and, 26–27
    reeds and, 26
    See also specific instruments

X

Xylophones, 9, 100

Z

Zithers, 62, 72, 90

PICTURE CREDITS

ABOUT THE AUTHOR

Stuart A. Kallen is the author of more than 250 nonfiction books for children and young adults. He has written extensively about science, the environment, music, culture, history, and folklore. In addition, Kallen has written award-winning children's videos and television scripts. In his spare time, he is a singer/songwriter/guitarist in San Diego.